GIVE THIS BOOK TO A
YANKEE!*

❧ THE LOCHLAINN SEABROOK COLLECTION ☙

Everything You Were Taught About the Civil War is Wrong, Ask a Southerner!
Everything You Were Taught About American Slavery is Wrong, Ask a Southerner!
Give This Book to a Yankee! A Southern Guide to the Civil War For Northerners
Honest Jeff and Dishonest Abe: A Southern Children's Guide to the Civil War
Confederacy 101: Amazing Facts You Never Knew About America's Oldest Political Tradition
Slavery 101: Amazing Facts You Never Knew About America's "Peculiar Institution"
The Great Yankee Coverup: What the North Doesn't Want You to Know About Lincoln's War!
Confederate Blood and Treasure: An Interview With Lochlainn Seabrook
Confederate Flag Facts
A Rebel Born: A Defense of Nathan Bedford Forrest - Confederate General, American Legend (winner of the 2011 Jefferson Davis Historical Gold Medal)
A Rebel Born: The Screenplay
Nathan Bedford Forrest: Southern Hero, American Patriot - Honoring a Confederate Icon and the Old South
The Quotable Nathan Bedford Forrest: Selections From the Writings and Speeches of the Confederacy's Most Brilliant Cavalryman
Give 'Em Hell Boys! The Complete Military Correspondence of Nathan Bedford Forrest
Forrest! 99 Reasons to Love Nathan Bedford Forrest
Saddle, Sword, and Gun: A Biography of Nathan Bedford Forrest For Teens
Nathan Bedford Forrest and the Battle of Fort Pillow: The True Story
The Quotable Jefferson Davis: Selections From the Writings and Speeches of the Confederacy's First President
The Quotable Alexander H. Stephens: Selections From the Writings and Speeches of the Confederacy's First Vice President
The Alexander H. Stephens Reader: Excerpts From the Works of a Confederate Founding Father
The Quotable Robert E. Lee: Selections From the Writings and Speeches of the South's Most Beloved Civil War General
The Old Rebel: Robert E. Lee As He Was Seen By His Contemporaries
The Articles of Confederation Explained: A Clause-by-Clause Study of America's First Constitution
The Constitution of the Confederate States of America Explained: A Clause-by-Clause Study of the South's Magna Carta
The Quotable Stonewall Jackson: Selections From the Writings and Speeches of the South's Most Famous General
Abraham Lincoln: The Southern View - Demythologizing America's Sixteenth President
The Unquotable Abraham Lincoln: The President's Quotes They Don't Want You To Know!
Lincolnology: The Real Abraham Lincoln Revealed in His Own Words - A Study of Lincoln's Suppressed, Misinterpreted, and Forgotten Writings and Speeches
The Great Impersonator! 99 Reasons to Dislike Abraham Lincoln
The Quotable Edward A. Pollard: Selections From the Writings of the Confederacy's Greatest Defender
Encyclopedia of the Battle of Franklin - A Comprehensive Guide to the Conflict that Changed the Civil War
Carnton Plantation Ghost Stories: True Tales of the Unexplained from Tennessee's Most Haunted Civil War House!
The McGavocks of Carnton Plantation: A Southern History - Celebrating One of Dixie's Most Noble Confederate Families and Their Tennessee Home
Jesus and the Law of Attraction: The Bible-Based Guide to Creating Perfect Health, Wealth, and Happiness Following Christ's Simple Formula
The Bible and the Law of Attraction: 99 Teachings of Jesus, the Apostles, and the Prophets
Christ Is All and In All: Rediscovering Your Divine Nature and the Kingdom Within
Jesus and the Gospel of Q: Christ's Pre-Christian Teachings As Recorded in the New Testament
Seabrook's Bible Dictionary of Traditional and Mystical Christian Doctrines
The Way of Holiness: The Story of Religion and Myth From the Cave Bear Cult to Christianity
Christmas Before Christianity: How the Birthday of the "Sun" Became the Birthday of the "Son"
Britannia Rules: Goddess-Worship in Ancient Anglo-Celtic Society - An Academic Look at the United Kingdom's Matricentric Spiritual Past
The Book of Kelle: An Introduction to Goddess-Worship and the Great Celtic Mother-Goddess Kelle, Original Blessed Lady of Ireland
The Goddess Dictionary of Words and Phrases: Introducing a New Core Vocabulary for the Women's Spirituality Movement
Princess Diana: Modern Day Moon-Goddess - A Psychoanalytical and Mythological Look at Diana Spencer's Life, Marriage, and Death (with Dr. Jane Goldberg)
Aphrodite's Trade: The Hidden History of Prostitution Unveiled
UFOs and Aliens: The Complete Guidebook
The Caudills: An Etymological, Ethnological, and Genealogical Study - Exploring the Name and National Origins of a European-American Family
The Blakeneys: An Etymological, Ethnological, and Genealogical Study - Uncovering the Mysterious Origins of the Blakeney Family and Name

Five-Star Books & Gifts With Five-Star Service!
SeaRavenPress.com

GIVE THIS BOOK TO A YANKEE!

A SOUTHERN GUIDE TO THE CIVIL WAR
For Northerners

A highly condensed version of the author's popular bestseller
Everything You Were Taught About the Civil War Is Wrong, Ask a Southerner!

LOCHLAINN SEABROOK
• JEFFERSON DAVIS HISTORICAL GOLD MEDAL WINNER •

FOREWORD BY KAREN COOPER

SEA RAVEN PRESS, NASHVILLE, TENNESSEE, USA

GIVE THIS BOOK TO A YANKEE!

Published by
Sea Raven Press, PO Box 1484, Spring Hill, Tennessee 37174-1484 USA
www.SeaRavenPress.com • searavenpress@gmail.com

Copyright © 2014 Lochlainn Seabrook
in accordance with U.S. and international copyright laws and regulations, as stated and protected under the Berne Union for the Protection of Literary and Artistic Property (Berne Convention), and the Universal Copyright Convention (the UCC). All rights reserved under the Pan-American and International Copyright Conventions.

First Sea Raven Press Edition: February 2014
ISBN: 978-0-9858632-9-6
Library of Congress Control Number: 2014931785

This work is the copyrighted intellectual property of Lochlainn Seabrook and has been registered with the Copyright Office at the Library of Congress in Washington, D.C., USA. No part of this work (including text, covers, drawings, photos, illustrations, maps, images, diagrams, etc.), in whole or in part, may be used, reproduced, stored in a retrieval system, or transmitted, in any form or by any means now known or hereafter invented, without written permission from the publisher. The sale, duplication, hire, lending, copying, digitalization, or reproduction of this material, in any manner or form whatsoever, is also prohibited, and is a violation of federal, civil, and digital copyright law, which provides severe civil and criminal penalties for any violations.

> Give This Book to a Yankee! A Southern Guide to the Civil War For Northerners, by Lochlainn Seabrook. Foreword by Karen Cooper. Includes endnotes and bibliographical references. Portions of this book have been adapted from the author's other works.

Front and back cover design and art, book design, layout, and interior art by Lochlainn Seabrook
Typography: Sea Raven Press Book Design
All images, graphic design, graphic art, and illustrations copyright © Lochlainn Seabrook
Cover image: "Battle of Pea Ridge," Library of Congress, 1889

The paper used in this book is acid-free and lignin-free. It has been certified by the Sustainable Forestry Initiative and the Forest Stewardship Council and meets all ANSI standards for archival quality paper.

PRINTED & MANUFACTURED IN OCCUPIED TENNESSEE, FORMER CONFEDERATE STATES OF AMERICA

· DEDICATION ·

*To any and all Yankees
who love and respect the South.*

· EPIGRAPH ·

Our enemy is not each other.
Our enemy is ignorance.

Lochlainn Seabrook, 2014

CONTENTS

Notes to the Reader - 8
Foreword, by Karen Cooper - 9
Introduction, by Lochlainn Seabrook - 11

1 The So-Called "Civil War" - 13
2 Who Launched the Civil War? - 17
3 What Was the Cause of the War? - 19
4 Differences Between South & North - 21
5 The Issue of Secession - 23
6 Nineteenth-Century Race Relations - 27
7 Slavery Myths - 30
8 Abolition - 36
9 Jefferson Davis - 37
10 Abraham Lincoln - 40
11 The Union's Naval Blockade - 43
12 The Emancipation Proclamation - 44
13 Lincoln's Black Colonization Plan - 49
14 Blacks & the Confederacy - 53
15 Blacks & the Union - 56
16 Civil War Prisons - 61
17 The Ku Klux Klan - 63
18 The Confederate Flag - 65
19 Reconstruction - 67

Notes - 70
Bibliography - 74
Meet the Author - 75

NOTES TO THE READER

☛ *Give This Book to a Yankee!*—a highly condensed "Reader's Digest" version of my much more detailed bestselling book, *Everything You Were Taught About the Civil War is Wrong, Ask a Southerner!*—is not meant to be a comprehensive compendium of the South's view of the "Civil War." For those seeking a fuller treatment of this fascinating and all-important subject, please see the latter work, as well as my book list on page 2. A true understanding of Lincoln's War is impossible without a thorough knowledge of the Southern perspective.

☛ As I heartily dislike the phrase "Civil War," for the reasons given in Chapter 1, its use in the subtitle of this book deserves an explanation. Today America's entire literary system refers to the conflict of 1861 using the Northern term the "Civil War," whether we in the South like it or not. Thus, as *all* book searches by readers, libraries, and retail outlets are now performed online, and as *all* bookstores categorize works from this period under the headings "Civil War" or "American Civil War," book publishers and authors who deal with this particular topic have little choice but to use these terms as well. If I were to refuse to use them, as some of my Southern colleagues have suggested, few people would ever find or read my books.

Add to this the fact that scarcely any non-Southerners have ever heard of the names we in the South use for the conflict, such as "The War for Southern Independence," "The War Against Northern Aggression," "The War for States' Rights," or my personal preference, "Lincoln's War." It only makes sense then to use the term "Civil War" in most commercial situations.

We should also consider that while today educated persons, particularly educated Southerners, all share an abhorrence for the phrase "Civil War," it was not always so. Confederates who lived through and even fought in the conflict regularly used the term throughout the 1860s, and even long after. Among them were Confederate generals such as Nathan Bedford Forrest, Richard Taylor, and Joseph E. Johnston, not to mention the Confederacy's vice president, Alexander H. Stephens. Even the Confederacy's highest official, President Jefferson Davis, used the term "Civil War," and in one case at least, as late as 1881—the year he wrote his brilliant exposition, *The Rise and Fall of the Confederate Government*.[1]

☛ In any study of early American history it is vitally important to bear in mind that in 1860 the platforms of the two major political parties were the opposite of what they are today. In other words, the Democrats of the mid 19th Century were conservatives, akin to the Republican Party of today, while the Republicans of the mid 19th Century were liberals, akin to the Democratic Party of today. Thus the Confederacy's Democratic president, Jefferson Davis, was a conservative (with libertarian leanings); the Union's Republican president, Abraham Lincoln, was a liberal (with socialistic leanings).[2]

FOREWORD

Award-winning author and historian Lochlainn Seabrook has done it again. He's given traditional Southerners yet another book that not only rectifies many of the notoriously false Yankee myths floating around out there, but one that makes Southerners genuinely proud to be Southern!

This brief work, provocatively entitled *Give This Book to a Yankee! A Southern Guide to the Civil War For Northerners*, is a loosely based distillation of his popular blockbuster *Everything You Were Taught About the Civil War is Wrong, Ask a Southerner!* Pared down several hundred pages for quick reading, as the title suggests, *Give This Book to a Yankee!* makes an excellent gift for your Northern friends, or even for fellow Southerners who have been inculcated with pro-North nonsense, and who need reeducating as to Dixie's authentic history.

The book's nineteen chapters cover the most salient aspects of what Mr. Seabrook likes to call "Lincoln's War," including such topics as the true cause behind the conflict, the legality of secession, race relations in the Old South and the Old North, myths about so-called "slavery," the real origins of the American abolition movement, Jeff Davis, Abe Lincoln, the Emancipation Proclamation, the treatment of blacks in the Confederate and Union armies, the KKK, Reconstruction, and much more. For scholars the book comes with over 200 endnotes and a bibliography.

Virginia Flagger Karen Cooper holding our bestselling book *Everything You Were Taught About the Civil War is Wrong, Ask a Southerner!*

Heavily researched and illustrated, this little book is an essential weapon anyone can use to defend Dixie and the Southern Cause, making it a must-have for traditional Southerners, Civil War buffs, and educators. Keep several copies on hand. You never know when you're going to bump into an unenlightened Yank or reconstructed Southerner!

Karen Cooper
The Virginia Flaggers
Richmond, Virginia
www.vaflaggers.blogspot.com

INTRODUCTION

If you are from outside the American South, particularly if you are from the Northeast, and are considering visiting or moving to Dixie, you owe it to yourself to read this book first. Why?

As you will learn from these pages, 150 years later the "Civil War" is still very much on the mind of most Southerners, and for good reason. For one thing, the conflict has always been seen as a direct assault on what we hold to be our country's most sacred document, the U.S. Constitution. We also view the War as an illegal invasion of a peace-loving agrarian society, by a meddlesome, self-righteous, and overbearing neighbor.

As a modern day Yankee, you might well ask what any of this has to do with you, someone who has no connection to the War. If you are heading down here to our section of the U.S., the answer is *everything*!

Though by Southern instinct and training we will welcome you, until we get to know where you stand on the War we will be wary. This is due to the fact that many from your region continue to follow in the footsteps of their pushy Union ancestors: upon arrival in the Southland, they immediately start trying to remake us into an exact copy of the North.

It usually starts with complaints about our "treasonous" Confederate monuments, cemeteries, and historical sites. These eventually turn into attempts at passing laws requiring the removal of Confederate statues, changing the names of Confederate parks, and banning the display of Confederate symbols on city-owned property. When these highly offensive ploys fail, some of the more South-loathing Yanks simply buy up and takeover entire sections of our towns, naming stores, shopping centers, and housing developments after famous Union officers—anything to aid in the age old movement of insulting, humiliating, demonizing, and Northernizing the South.

Were they alive today, anti-South advocates like Abraham Lincoln, Ulysses S. Grant, and William T. Sherman would certainly be proud of such die-hard Unionists. However, this nefarious maneuver did not work in 1861, and it does not work today. For you cannot destroy an idea that still lives in the hearts and minds of millions of Southerners. And what is that idea? It is the traditional conservative concept of a small limited central government overseen by the free people of all-powerful sovereign states; in other words, the very government Lincoln pretended he wanted but, in fact, tried to destroy: "A government of the people, by the people, for the people."

Of course, we do not blame y'all for wanting to come South. It is a universally acknowledged fact that our weather is better, our economy is stronger, our women are prettier, our men are politer, our children are nicer, our accent is sweeter, our sports teams are greater, our land is grander, our schools are superior, our food is tastier, our society is more diverse, and our history is more interesting than what you find up North. Ever hear of "Northern cooking," "Northern hospitality," "Northern charm," "Northern pride," "Northern rock," or "retiring up North"? Dixie is a totally unique American culture, and we aim to keep it that way, thank you.

Consider this: when a Southerner travels to the North, she does not try to change everything around her to suit her Southern sensibilities. She accepts things as they are. And when her business is done, she leaves her Yankee friends with a "bless you," and heads back home. All we ask is the same courtesy: accept us as we are, or as our beloved President Jefferson Davis once said to the Union: "Let us alone!"

This book will teach you why this is so important to us, and why it is that the Northerner has no right to feel superior to the Southerner. It will reveal to you why a Yank should always come here with a sense of courteousness, good will, and deference toward Dixie and her gallant, gracious, and fiercely independent people.

Learn our ways; accept them and respect them before you judge. For once an intelligent Yankee learns the Truth about the "Civil War," his hostility toward the South quickly turns to empathy, and he himself becomes a Southerner at heart. This has happened to thousands of Northerners over the years. It might could just happen to you.

Lochlainn Seabrook
February 2014
Nashville, Tennessee, USA

1

THE SO-CALLED "CIVIL WAR"

☛ The term "Civil War" is a deceptive misnomer, invented by the Union to mislead the public by disguising the true character of the War. The so-called "Civil War" was fought by two separate, autonomous, and legally formed republics or countries: the Confederate States of America (C.S.A.) and the United States of America (U.S.A.). Therefore it was not a true "civil war," as Webster defines it: "a war between opposing groups of citizens of the same country."[3]

☛ While in the 1860s (and thereafter) some Confederate leaders did indeed occasionally use the phrase "civil war," among traditional Southerners today it is generally shunned as an inaccurate and purposefully deceitful Northern term.[4]

☛ Today there are many preferred Southern terms for the American "Civil War," the most popular being: "The War for Southern Independence," "The War for States' Rights," and "The War Against Northern Aggression." As a Southern historian, however, my personal preference is "Lincoln's War," as it is the most historically accurate.[5]

☛ The South today is not still "fighting the Civil War." But she *is* still fighting for the principles that her 19th-Century ancestors fought and died for: strict constitutionality, states' rights, a small limited central government, conservative Jeffersonian political ideals, free trade, capitalism, fiscal responsibility, and traditional family and religious values.[6]

☛ Southerners believe that it is the North who is still fighting the War. Why? Because each year pro-North publishers continue to release hundreds of propagandized books supporting the Lincoln administration and the Union while denigrating the Davis administration and the Confederacy. All of this only could only have one purpose: to continue breeding animosity toward the South and her people.[7]

☛ Long prior to the Civil War, during the conflict, and long after, we Southerners have only asked to be left alone. We have never had any desire to interfere with the North, and only ask that the North respect our privacy and rights in return. However, the naturally nosy Yankee has never been able to fully honor this agreement, and to this day he still busies himself butting into the affairs of Dixie.[8]

☛ In contrast to the North, the effects of Lincoln's War are still very much alive in the South. This is because most of the War's battles were fought here, where the remnants of the damage are still clearly visible.[9]

☛ During the War Union troops not only cruelly displaced and rendered homeless millions of innocent Southern civilians, they also wantonly destroyed billions of dollars of Southern real estate, including: homes, businesses, railroads, farms, plantations, and factories. Even Southern churches, schools, universities, hospitals, and libraries were not spared the torch. What was the purpose of such mindless and illegal terrorism against fellow Americans, and all noncombatants?[10]

☛ Union troops committed untold numbers of heinous crimes against Southerners of all races, including: illegal arrest, imprisonment, torture, and murder. Southern women, both white and black, were routinely subjected to humiliation, physical abuse, and even rape in their own homes.[11]

☛ Yankee officers, like William T. Sherman, enjoyed bragging about their destruction of Southern towns, some, like Meridian, Mississippi, that were unnecessarily burned to the ground, turning thousands into wandering, starving refugees. Carl Sandburg, no friend of the South, rightly referred to the Yankees' impact on Dixie as a "human slaughterhouse."[12]

☛ Since Lincoln's War was fought mainly in the South, most Northerners never witnessed the true horrors of the conflict. Indeed, the majority of the North was never even remotely touched by the War. Yet nearly every Southerner experienced Lincoln's savagery firsthand.[13]

☛ It is because of this that the memory of Lincoln's War has been kept alive, and transferred from generation to generation across the South for the past century and a half.[14]

☛ Though the total cost of the Civil War is estimated at about $150 billion in today's currency, the true damage Lincoln and his troops inflicted on the South has never been properly assessed, nor will it ever be. It is too great. The expenditure in Southern blood and treasure is beyond counting.[15]

☛ While the North gives a figure of 329,000 Confederate deaths, we Southern historians more accurately count at least 2 million Southern deaths total. This includes both combatants and noncombatants, and all races—at least 1 million of which were Southern whites (out of 8 million) and 1 million of which were Southern blacks (out of 4 million). Casualty rates for Southern reds (Native-Americans), Southern browns (Hispanic-Americans), and Southern yellows (Asian-Americans) were never counted, and so are unavailable; but we can be sure they numbered in the many thousands.[16]

☛ Though the North has long taught that the War was "necessary," in the South we deem it "the most unnecessary war in world history." For not only was secession *legal*, but Lincoln did not preserve the *voluntary* union created by the Founding Fathers. And neither did he end slavery—which was only finally abolished eight months after he died under the Thirteenth Amendment. What then was the purpose? To prove that the North had more military might than the South, a point that Southerners never once disputed?[17]

☛ Union official William H. Seward once referred to Lincoln's War as an "irrepressible conflict," insinuating that the North had no choice but to take up arms against Dixie. Southerners, however, call this just another damnable Yankee lie, for before the conflict even started, our president, the honorable Confederate leader Jefferson Davis, sent one peace commission after another to the U.S. White House in an attempt to prevent bloodshed. And later, during the War, he did everything in his power to draw the conflict to a close as soon as possible.[18]

☛ All of this was to no avail: Lincoln refused all invitations to meet with Confederate peace-makers until he was assured of a Union victory. This did not occur until a mere two months before war's end, when he deigned to meet with several Confederate diplomats on February 3, 1865, at the Hampton Roads Conference in Virginia. To the South this fact alone proves that Lincoln was never interested in peace or even in resolving the conflict legally, in a court of law, as it should have been. Instead, it clearly demonstrates that he wanted and needed war.[19]

☛ While the North "won" the War, this does not mean that it was in the right. As Napoleon long ago declared, "God favors the side with the biggest battalions," and we here in Dixie agree. The South had one third the men, money, resources, and supplies, basically assuring the outcome in the Union's favor from the very beginning. All the North proved was that it had the biggest battalions, not that it had the moral high ground.[20]

☛ "The South was right," and it had known this from the start, just as Southern defender John A. Richardson proclaimed in 1914.[21] Why? Because the Confederacy fought to preserve the Constitution while the Union fought against it. The truth is that Davis allowed and even encouraged civil rights during the War, while Lincoln restricted and actually destroyed civil rights, a difference that could only tip the scales northward—which is precisely what occurred.[22]

2

WHO LAUNCHED THE CIVIL WAR?

☛ Though the South indeed fired the first shot at the Battle of Fort Sumter, South Carolina, on April 12, 1861, this does not mean that she started the Civil War.[23]

☛ Even before Lincoln was inaugurated into office on March 4, 1861, he had begun concocting a truly devious plot to trick the Confederacy into initiating the fight at Fort Sumter. This involved planning a mission to resupply starving Union troops still stationed on the island in Charleston Harbor. His alleged goal was to allow them to remain for as long as possible to defend the stronghold against South Carolina, who having seceded, was now claiming the island fort as her own.[24]

☛ Yet the majority of the Northern people, most Yankee politicians, and nearly the entire Lincoln administration, were all against the idea of resupplying Fort Sumter. Instead, everyone from the greatly respected Yankee General Winfield Scott down to Lincoln's secretary of war, Simon Cameron, urged the president to simply evacuate the fort in order to avoid a "civil war." What they did not realize, however, was that Lincoln wanted war. It was just that he did not want to be the one to start it.[25]

☛ Meanwhile, the Southern states began threatening the North with military action if Lincoln resupplied Fort Sumter, which is exactly what the crafty Illinoisan wanted.[26]

☛ In truth, Lincoln's Fort Sumter troops were anything but "starving," for they had been regularly and generously fed by the charitable folks of Charleston, who had daily sent out "a boat load of food supplies, fresh meats, fowls, fruits, vegetables, etc." to the men. The "starving Union troops" story was, in fact, a ruse.[27]

☛ Seeing the Federal fleet moving through Charleston Harbor toward Fort Sumter, Confederate troops let loose their cannon. For a full thirty-six hours they bombarded the island, expecting at any moment to receive enemy fire. But the expected Yankee response never came. Why? Because Lincoln had ordered his men not to respond. It was all a hoax, one meant to goad the Confederacy into firing the first shot.[28]

☛ The fraud, wholly supported by Lincoln, instigated by his secretary of the navy Gideon Welles, and detailed by Welles' assistant Gustavus Fox, worked brilliantly: the South, boiling over with animus for the interfering Northern military machine, had taken the bait, forever after becoming known to the world as the one who "fired the first shot."[29]

☛ Both Lincoln and his biographers John G. Nicolay and John Hay later acknowledged the plot that tainted the reputation of the South and launched the most bloody conflict ever fought on U.S. soil. But it was too late: the myth that the South had been the aggressor and that the North was merely "trying to defend the U.S. flag," had become a permanent part of American folklore.[30]

☛ Six years later, Southern journalist and author Edward A. Pollard wrote: "The battle of Sumter had been brought on by the Washington Government by a trick too dishonest and shallow to account for the immense display of sentiment in the North that ensued. The event afforded indeed to many politicians in the North a most flimsy and false excuse for loosing passions of hate against the South that had all along been festering in the concealment of their hearts."[31]

3

WHAT WAS THE CAUSE OF THE WAR?

☞ There was really only one primary cause of the Civil War, and it was the same political battle that continues today: the eternal struggle between conservatism and liberalism, or what Confederate Vice President Alexander H. Stephens called "constitutionalism" and "consolidationism."[32]

☞ As today, in 1861 most conservatives or constitutionalists lived in the South, while most liberals or consolidationists lived in the North.[33]

☞ In essence, Southern conservatives wanted to preserve the Constitution as it was written by the Founding Fathers, while Northern liberals wanted to alter it to fit their progressive even socialist-leaning agenda. The matter thus came down to whether or not to maintain or overthrow the Constitution.[34]

☞ In her effort to leave the Union, the South fought to preserve the Constitution—which includes the tacit guarantee of both states' rights and secession (see the Ninth and Tenth Amendments).[35]

☞ In her effort to prevent the South from leaving the Union, the North fought to overturn the Constitution.[36]

☞ Lincoln could not admit this publically, so he gave numerous other reasons for trying to destroy the Confederacy, including money[37] and, most famously, to "preserve the Union."[38]

☛ There were a number of other ancillary reasons for the War, but none of them had anything to do with so-called "slavery." Where does slavery fit in then? It doesn't, and never did[39]—just as both President Davis and President Lincoln declared.

☛ Here is what Davis had to say on the matter: "The truth remains intact and incontrovertible, that the existence of African servitude was in no wise the cause of the conflict, but only an incident. In the later controversies that arose, however, its effect in operating as a lever upon the passions, prejudices, or sympathies of mankind, was so potent that it has been spread like a thick cloud over the whole horizon of historic truth."[40]

☛ Here is what Lincoln said about the true cause of the War: "My enemies pretend I am now carrying on this war for the sole purpose of abolition. So long as I am President, it shall be carried on for the sole purpose of restoring the Union."[41] In other words, those who today claim that the War was over slavery, Lincoln would call his "enemies."

☛ Why did the conservative South want to maintain the original Constitution, and even reinstate many of the ideas found in America's first constitution, the Articles of Confederation? Because the original U.S.—known as "the Confederacy," or more precisely as "the Confederate States of America," from 1781 to 1789—was built around the idea of small limited central government that was overseen by autonomous all-powerful sovereign states, the goal of all true conservatives, traditionalists, and libertarians.[42]

And this is why, of course, the seceding Southern states adopted the name "the Confederate States of America" for their new republic in 1861. It was an effort to preserve and continue the Founders' first U.S. republic, not an attempt to destroy it, as pro-North writers claim.[43]

☛ Why did the liberal North want to overthrow the original Constitution, rewrite and amend various clauses, and even add new ones? Because they could not achieve their dream of big government under it: the original Constitution placed too many restrictions on the central government, preventing governmental centralization and expansion, the dream of all true liberals, progressives, and Marxists.[44]

4

DIFFERENCES BETWEEN SOUTH & NORTH

☞ Today many Northerners like to pretend that the South and the North are two equal, compatible, homogenous, even interchangeable regions, with more in common than not. This is indeed what many would like to believe. But in fact the opposite is true, has always been true, and, if Southerners have anything to say about it, will forever remain true.[45]

☞ Prior to the "Civil War" the North was primarily industrial, institutional, urban, nationalistic, liberal, radical, conformist, agnostic, Catholic, progressive, business oriented, and publicly schooled. To the Yankee mind the Union was a purely commercial entity, a single monolithic democracy by which that region could profit through tariffs, bounties, and "sectional aggrandizement."[46]

☞ In contrast to this stance, one known as "Yankeeism" here in the South, Dixie was mainly agricultural, personal, rural, localistic, conservative, Constitutional, individualistic, highly religious, Protestant, traditional, family oriented, and home-schooled. To the Southern mind the Union was a moral social order, a "friendly association" of states held together by "good faith," the "exchanges of equity and comity," and the concept of states' rights.[47]

☛ There were a number of other social and cultural differences, however. As the South saw it, Northerners were discourteous and reserved, while they themselves were well mannered and emotional.⁴⁸

☛ Northerners were greedy, shrewd, and materialistic, while Southerners were generous, hospitable, and spiritual.⁴⁹

☛ Northern society was prim, proper, and fast-paced, Southern society was relaxed, informal, and leisurely.⁵⁰

☛ While Northerners considered themselves Americans, Southerners considered themselves Southerners.⁵¹

☛ This purely Southern sense of identity, combined with the sectional strife they were continually engaged in with their Yankee neighbors, eventually developed into what would come to be called the "Confederate Cause": Southerners' desire to maintain their own way of life, traditional American values founded upon the principles of the Declaration of Independence, penned by Southern hero and Founding Father Thomas Jefferson (a school of thought known today as Jeffersonianism, which combines aspects of conservatism, paleoconservatism, traditionalism, libertarianism, and Tea Partyism). Thus, in the Old South one was either pro-South and anti-North or pro-North and anti-South. There was no middle ground.⁵²

☛ It was just such sociopolitical differences, along with hundreds of others (including the agricultural South's centuries old economic enslavement to the North's domineering industrial interests), that eventually helped lead the country into war.⁵³

5

THE ISSUE OF SECESSION

☛ The American right of secession is legal today, it was legal in 1860, and it will continue to be legal as long as the Constitution exists.[54]

☛ America herself was born of secession (from Britain) and is therefore a secessionist country, just as the Declaration of Independence affirms: "When, in the course of human events, it becomes necessary for one people to dissolve the political bands which have connected them with another . . . a decent respect to the opinions of mankind requires that they should declare the causes which impel them to the separation. . . . We, therefore, the representatives of the United States of America, in general Congress assembled . . . do, in the name, and by the authority of the good people of these colonies, solemnly publish and declare, that these united colonies are, and of right ought to be, free and independent states."[55]

☛ To officially form the U.S., the Founding Fathers had to allow a colony or state to enter the Union, that is, *accede*. This in turn meant that a state or colony also had the right to leave the Union, that is, *secede*.[56] These two rights were not spelled out in our earliest national documents because they were so well-known, so well understood, and so well accepted by every politician and citizen at the time that they were simply taken for granted. Actually, up until 1865, secession was the most frequently discussed political issue in both the United States and the Confederate States.[57] And so they were tacitly included in a body of rights known as "states' rights."[58]

☛ Thus Article Two of our first constitution, the Articles of Confederation of 1777, reads: "Each state retains its sovereignty, freedom, and independence, and every power, jurisdiction, and right, which is not by this Confederation expressly delegated to the United States, in Congress assembled."[59]

☛ When the Articles of Confederation were replaced in 1791, the Founders maintained the idea of states' rights (which included the assumed right of secession), carrying them forward into the Constitution of the United States. Article Four, Section Four of that document reads: "The United States shall guarantee to every state in this Union a republican form of government."[60] The word *republican* was an 18th-Century term for *confederacy*: a small limited government whose power rests with the people, and whose states are sovereign and which possess full states' rights, including the rights to accede and secede.[61]

☛ To ensure that the states would never lose their individual rights to the central government, they were permanently set forth in the Tenth Amendment of the Bill of Rights: "The powers not delegated to the United States by the Constitution [see Article Four, Section Four], nor prohibited by it to the States, are reserved to the States respectively, or to the people."[62]

☛ Before his war on the Constitution and the American people, Abraham Lincoln was not only aware of the right of secession, he wholeheartedly supported it. Here, for example, is what he said on January 12, 1848, in a speech before the U.S. House of Representatives: "Any people anywhere, being inclined and having the power, have the right to rise up, and shake off the existing government, and form a new one that suits them better. This is a most valuable, a most sacred right—a right which, we hope and believe, is to liberate the world. Nor is this right confined to cases in which the whole people of an existing government may choose to exercise it. Any portion of such people that can may revolutionize, and make their own of so much of the territory as they inhabit."[63]

☛ Just a little over a decade later, after the 1860 secession of the first Southern state (South Carolina), Lincoln began calling secession a form of "anarchy," a "despotism," and an "ingenious sophistry" that would eventually lead to the "overthrow of the [U.S.] government" and the "destruction of the

Union."⁶⁴ What caused him to reverse his stance on the right of secession?

☛ Though Lincoln knew that secession was legal in 1860, now that he was president it no longer suited his liberal agenda: to enlarge and further consolidate power in the central government. To achieve this goal, what was then called the "American System," the states would need to be stripped of as many states' rights as possible, including the right of secession.⁶⁵

☛ Secession being a perfectly legal and constitutionally permanent right of each state, this makes the Civil War illegal and Lincoln a war criminal. This fact, part of what I call "The Great Yankee Coverup,"⁶⁶ has been withheld from the public since the start of the conflict in 1861, and keeping it concealed has become the obsession of every pro-North, anti-South writer, historian, and politician ever since.⁶⁷

☛ Nonetheless, we cannot escape authentic history. Here, for instance, is what America's Founding Father and third president Thomas Jefferson had to say about secession during his First Inaugural Address in 1801: "If there be any among us who would wish to dissolve the Union or to change its republican form, let them stand undisturbed as monuments of the safety with which error of opinion may be tolerated where reason is left free to combat it."⁶⁸

☛ In June 1816, now a former U.S. president, Jefferson wrote a letter to William Crawford that read in part: "If any state in the Union will declare that it prefers separation to a continuance in the Union, I have no hesitation in saying, 'Let us separate.'"⁶⁹

☛ In 1860 a truly stunning number of Northerners agreed with both Jefferson and the "Cotton States" (that is, the South), that secession was indeed lawful, and that, under the circumstances, it was entirely appropriate for the South to part company with the Union. One of these was Yankee abolitionist and New York *Tribune* owner Horace Greeley, who, in the November 10, 1860, issue, wrote: "And now, if the Cotton States consider the value of the Union debatable, we maintain their perfect right to discuss it. Nay, we hold with Jefferson to the inalienable right of communities to alter or abolish forms of government that have become oppressive or injurious; and if the Cotton States shall decide that they can do better out of the Union than in it, we insist on letting them go in peace. The right to secede may be a revolutionary one, but it exists nevertheless; and we do not see how one party can have a right to do what another party has a right to prevent. We must ever resist the asserted right of any State to remain in the Union and nullify or defy the laws thereof; to withdraw from the Union is quite another matter. And whenever a considerable section of our Union shall deliberately resolve to go out, we shall resist all coercive measures designed to keep it in. We hope never to live in a republic, whereof one section is pinned to the residue with bayonets."[70]

☛ In the end, Lincoln's assertion that the act of secession was nothing more than a "rebellion" against the Union was both false and legally inaccurate. For as Jefferson Davis pointed out, the Southern states were "the sovereign parties to the compact of union," and thus they "had the reserved power to secede from it whenever it should be found not to answer the ends for which it was established." In other words, sovereigns cannot rebel because there is nothing to rebel against. They are free entities, with the power to come and go as they please, when and how they please.[71]

☛ Like dictators before and after him, Lincoln preferred to live in an *involuntary* Union in which its separate states were "pinned to the residue with bayonets," as Greeley put it. The South preferred to live in a *voluntary* Union where states' rights were honored and maintained, allowing for the free and unimpeded ingress and egress of the separate states, just as the Ninth and Tenth Amendments tacitly promise.[72]

☛ Which side was in the right then? According to both the Founding Fathers and the U.S. Constitution, the South. For secession was, and still is, entirely legal. As mentioned, this is what makes Lincoln's War, the "Civil War," illegal, and it is what makes Lincoln a war criminal.[73]

6

NINETEENTH-CENTURY RACE RELATIONS

☛ Though you have been taught otherwise, the truth is that American race relations have always been worse in the North than in the South, and the same is still true today. Observations of this fact were being made by reliable eyewitnesses as far back as the 1700s and 1800s.[74]

☛ Alexis de Tocqueville was not the first, but only one of many, who noted that in early America white racism was far more severe in the North than in the South. During his tour of the states in 1831 the French aristocrat summed up his impressions this way: "Whosoever has inhabited the United States must have perceived that in those parts of the Union [i.e., in the North] in which the negroes are no longer slaves, they have in no wise drawn nearer to the whites. On the contrary, the prejudice of the race appears to be stronger in the States which have abolished slavery [i.e., in the North] than in those where it still exists [i.e., in the South]; and nowhere is it so intolerant as in those States [i.e., in the West] where servitude never has been known. . . . In the South, where slavery still exists, the negroes are less carefully kept apart; they sometimes share the labour and the recreations of the whites; the whites consent to intermix with them to a certain extent, and although the legislation treats them more harshly, the habits of the [Southern] people are more tolerant and compassionate."[75]

☛ In the 1840s English writer James Silk Buckingham wrote that "the prejudice of colour is not nearly so strong in the South as in the North."[76]

☛ In 1830 here is how Robert Young Hayne, a South Carolina senator, described the treatment of Southern blacks who moved to the so-called "abolitionist North" in search of "freedom": "There does not exist on the face of the whole earth, a population so poor, so wretched, so vile, so loathsome, so utterly destitute of all the comforts, conveniences, and decencies of life, as the unfortunate blacks of Philadelphia, and New York and Boston. Liberty has been to them the greatest of calamities, the heaviest of curses. Sir, I have had some opportunities of making comparison between the condition of the free negroes of the North, and the slaves of the South, and the comparison has left not only an indelible impression of the superior advantages of the latter, but has gone far to reconcile me to slavery itself. Never have I felt so forcibly that touching description, 'the foxes have holes, and the birds of the air have nests, but the Son of Man hath not where to lay his head,' as when I have seen this unhappy race, naked and houseless, almost starving in the streets, and abandoned by all the world. Sir, I have seen, in the neighborhood of one of the most moral, religious and refined cities of the North, a family of free blacks driven to the caves of the rocks, and there obtaining a precarious subsistence from charity and plunder."[77]

☛ In 1835 Virginian James Madison met with English author Harriet Martineau, and regaled her with stories about how the Northern states erected numerous barriers in an attempt to thwart Negro emigration.[78]

☛ In 1841, after traveling through Philadelphia, an English Quaker, Joseph Sturge, met with former Illinois Governor Edward Coles. Writes Sturge: "In the course of conversation, the Governor spoke of the prejudice against colour prevailing here as much stronger than in the slave States [the South]. I may add, from my own observation, and much concurring testimony, that Philadelphia appears to be the metropolis of this odious prejudice, and that there is probably no city in the known world, where dislike, amounting to hatred of the coloured population, prevails more than in the city of brotherly love!"[79]

☛ After a visit to New York City, English writer Edward Dicey recorded his observations concerning Yankee racism and Northern blacks. In the North, Dicey noted in 1863: "Everywhere and at all seasons the coloured people form a separate community. In the public streets you hardly ever see a coloured person in company with a white, except in the capacity of servant. . . . On board the river steamboats, the commonest and homeliest of working [white] men has a right to dine, and does dine, at the public meals; but, for coloured passengers, there is always a separate table. At the great [Northern] hotels there is, as with us [in England], a servants' table, but the coloured servants are not allowed to dine in common with the white. At the inns, in the barbers' shops, on board the steamers, and in most hotels, the servants are more often than not coloured people. . . . White [Northern] servants will not associate with black on terms of equality. . . . I hardly ever remember seeing a black employed as shopman, or placed in any post of responsibility. As a rule, the blacks you meet in the Free [that is, Northern] States are shabbily, if not squalidly dressed; and, as far as I could learn, the instances of black men having made money by trade in the North, are very few in number."⁸⁰

☞ In his 1918 book *American Negro Slavery*, Ulrich B. Phillips writes: "Fanny Kemble [the famed white British actress], in her more vehement style, wrote of the negroes in the North: 'They are not slaves indeed, but they are pariahs, debarred from every fellowship save with their own despised race, scorned by the lowest white ruffian in your streets, not tolerated even by the foreign menials in your kitchen. They are free certainly, but they are also degraded, rejected, the offscum and the offscouring of the very dregs of your society. . . .'"⁸¹

☞ On August 15, 1862, a black Massachusetts justice of the peace, John S. Rock, made the following remarks about white racism there. According to Rock, the Bay State did not compare favorably with Southern states, such as South Carolina: " . . . it is ten times more difficult for a colored mechanic to get employment [here in Boston] than in Charleston . . . . if we don't like that state of things, there is an appropriation to colonize [deport] us."⁸²

7

SLAVERY MYTHS

☛ The North has long enjoyed referring to Southern slavery as the "peculiar institution." But actually there is nothing "peculiar" about it, nor is it specifically Southern.[83]

☛ An institution that has been found on every continent and among nearly every civilization from earliest recorded history right into present-day America can hardly be considered "peculiar." In fact, as this chapter reveals, it would be more appropriately and accurately called the "standard institution."[84]

☛ To begin with, it is a well established fact, acknowledged even by liberal white and black historians, that Africans were practicing slavery on each other millennia before the first European slave ships visited West Africa. Among the early African peoples who practiced slavery were the Yoruba of western Nigeria, the Fon of Dahomey, and the Fanti and Asante (or Ashanti) of Ghana. Entire African civilizations were built on and maintained by slavery, using some of the world's cruelest and most inhumane forms of bondage known. Slavery continues unabated across the African continent to this day, with some 200,000 African children alone being enslaved by other Africans each year.[85]

☛ No one knows who actually invented slavery, of course, but we do know that it dates from prehistory, was once universally accepted around the world, and that at one time it was found on every continent, in every single nation, and among every people, race, religion, and ethnic group. As such it must certainly be counted as one of humanity's most ancient social institutions, and an essential feature of both society and economics.[86]

☞ This makes slavery a natural byproduct of human culture, placing it alongside our other oldest human social institutions: hunting and gathering, religion, marriage, warfare, puberty rites, funerary rites, and prostitution. Indeed, many anthropologists consider slavery not an indication of barbarity, but an early sign of civilization: its emergence meant that humans had begun to enslave rather than kill one another.[87]

☞ From its appearance in the prehistoric mists of time, slavery went onto be employed by the Mesopotamians (ancient Iraqis), Indians, Chinese, ancient Egyptians, Hebrews, Greeks, and Romans. In the pre-Columbian Americas slavery became an integral part of such Native-American peoples as the Maya, Aztec, and Inca, who depended on large scale slave labor in warfare and farming.[88]

☞ Both the earliest known slave traders and the earliest known slaves were Caucasians: the Babylonians, Assyrians, Sumerians, Akkadians, Mesopotamians, Phoenicians, Egyptians, Mycenaeans, Arameans, East Indians, Chaldeans, Hittites, Scythians, Persians, Arabians, and Hebrews—at some point in their history—all either enslaved other whites or were themselves enslaved by other whites.[89]

☞ The reality is that slavery is a ubiquitous worldwide phenomenon, one that stubbornly persists into modern times, and which dates far back into the fog of prehistory in all lands, and among all races, ethnic groups, religions, societies, and peoples. All of us then, no matter what our race, color, or nationality, have ancestors who were once in bondage and who once held others in bondage. *We are all descendants of slaves and slave owners.*[90]

☞ Concerning American slavery specifically, here are the facts: the American slave trade got its start in Boston, Massachusetts, in 1638, when Captain William Pierce brought New England's first shipload of Africans from the West Indies aboard the Salem vessel *Desire*. As for American slavery, this too began in Massachusetts, which became the first state to legalize the Yankees' "peculiar institution" in 1641.[91]

☞ From Massachusetts, both the slave trade and slavery spread like wildfire across the Northeast, with major slave-trading ports sprouting up not only in Boston, but in Bristol and Newport, Rhode Island; Baltimore and Annapolis, Maryland; Philadelphia, Pennsylvania; and our nation's capital, Washington, D.C.[92]

☛ Many of New England's most famous families derived their wealth from Yankee slavery, including: the Cabots (ancestors of Massachusetts Senators Henry Cabot Lodge Sr. and Henry Cabot Lodge Jr.), the Belchers, the Waldos (ancestors of Ralph Waldo Emerson), the Faneuils (after whom Boston's Faneuil Hall is named), the Royalls, the Pepperells (after whom the town of Pepperell, Massachusetts, is named), the DeWolfs (at least 500,000 descendants of their slaves are alive today), the Champlains (after whom Lake Champlain is named), the Ellerys, the Gardners (after whom Boston's Isabella Stewart Gardner Museum is named), the Malbones, the Robinsons, the Crowninshields (after whom Crowninshield Island, Massachusetts, is named), and the Browns (after whom Rhode Island's Brown University is named). The slave trading Royall family, who made millions from their slave plantations in Antigua, donated money and land to what would become the Harvard Law School. The educational center still uses a seal from the Royall family crest.[93]

☛ It was New York City, however, that eventually came to be the main port of exit and entry for America's great slave ships. This is why, by 1720, New York had become one of the largest slaveholding states in the North, with 4,000 slaves against a white population of only 31,000.[94] New York ended up practicing slavery longer than any other state North or South: from 1626 to 1865, a span of 239 years. This is 123 years longer than the South practiced it. Yet it is the South which is still blamed for the institution![95]

☛ New York City is today America's largest and wealthiest municipality for one and only one primary reason: for centuries it served as the literal heart of North America's slaving industry. Many of the most famous New York names, in fact—names such as the Lehman Brothers, John Jacob Astor, Junius and Pierpont Morgan, Charles Tiffany, Archibald Gracie, and many others—are only known today because of the tremendous riches their families made from the town's "peculiar institution."[96]

☛ The reality is that it was the North's heavy dependence on the Yankee slave trade and on selling slaves to the South, that helped precipitate the "Civil War": in March 1861 the Southern Confederacy adopted its

Constitution, which included a clause banning slave trading with foreign nations. "Foreign nations," of course, included the U.S. The North panicked, deciding it was better to beat the South into submission than allow her to cut off one of the Yankees' primary economic arteries. Big government liberal Lincoln, the only 1860 presidential candidate who pledged not to interfere with slavery, and who was put into office by Northern industrialists using profits from the Northern slave trade, launched the "Civil War" in April, just a few weeks later.[97]

☛ Among those Northerners most interested in the continuation of slavery were New York's "Wall Street Boys," that is, the Northern business establishment, which had bankrolled Lincoln's first (and later his second) presidential campaign using money they had made primarily from the Yankee slave trade. There was also the Boston elite, who made it known that they were quite willing to make huge concessions to the South in the interest of making money.[98]

☛ Is it any wonder then that in his First Inaugural Address, March, 4 1861, Lincoln promised not to disturb slavery, or that American slavery did not come to a final end until December 6, 1865 (eight months after Lincoln's death), with the passage of the Thirteenth Amendment?[99]

☛ Slavery was finally phased out in the North (it was never formally abolished),[100] not because the always materialistic Victorian Yankee began to feel shame or guilt, but because it became unprofitable. And it only became unprofitable due to the North's largely rocky sandy soil and short cold summers, which made the region unsuitable for large-scale farming.[101]

☛ Another factor, of course, was Northern white racism: most 18th- and 19th-Century Yanks simply preferred to live in an all-white society, free from what white supremacist Lincoln called the "natural disgust" engendered in whites at the mere thought of the two races mixing together. And so the Northern states "abolished" slavery in the late 1700s and early 1800s—though the institution continued illegally there, with the tacit approval of the U.S. government, until after the "Civil War."[102]

☛ It was in this way that when the white North grew tired of dealing with blacks and slavery, yet desperately needing a way to keep the institution alive and its wealth stream flowing northward, she pushed slavery south on a mostly unwilling populace, one that had been trying to abolish it since the 1700s. Why force slavery on the South specifically? It killed two birds with one stone: first, it ridded the Northeast of the unwanted black man, and second, it took advantage of Dixie's year-round temperate climate, massive broad flat fields, and rich alluvial soil, all which were far more conducive to the large-scale farming needed to grow the North's biggest money-making crop: King Cotton, the lynchpin of New England's great textile mills, whose profits were used to send more Yankee slave ships to Africa.[103]

☞ Since the true definition of a slave is one who is, like livestock, owned and controlled for life by another, has no legal rights, must work without pay, and cannot purchase his freedom, the type of bondage practiced in the South was clearly not "slavery."[104]

☞ What *was* practiced in the South was a form of servitude, a type of vassalage in which the so-called "master-slave" relationship was more akin to "employer-employee"; an apprentice like relationship of limited duration, in which the "employee" was paid a wage and could hire himself out to others.[105]

☞ The Southern "slave" was thus more properly called a "servant," for not only was he protected by a litany of human and civil rights, but he was given Sundays, evenings, and holidays off (often he had the entire week free between Christmas and New Year's Day), while extracurricular free time was always set aside for birthday celebrations, barbeques, weddings, fishing and hunting jaunts, parties, balls, prayer meetings, square dancing, and funerals, among numerous other activities. He worked less hours per week than a modern office worker, and had all of his needs paid for by his "employer": food, shelter, clothing, and healthcare, supplied from birth to the end of his service, or his life. Above all, he could purchase his freedom. These things, and more, set the Southern servant completely apart from the Northen slave.[106]

☞ Only a tiny minority of Southerners ever owned "slaves": less than 4.8 percent in 1860, the peak period of the institution. Thus the idea of a "slave-owning majority" and the notion that "slavery was the cornerstone of the Confederacy" are both patent perversions of the truth.[107]

☞ Southern "slaves" were considered members of their "owner's" family and were registered as such at the time of purchase.[108] Northern slaves, however, were registered on the same list as farm animals and appliances.[109]

☞ Slave owning was not exclusively a European-American profession. Right up to the time of Lincoln's War untold thousands of Native-Americans and African-Americans also owned slaves. The former group owned more on average than white slave owners, while the latter group included black families like the Metoyers, an anti-abolition family from Louisiana that owned huge numbers of black slaves; in their case, at least 400. At about $1,500 a piece, their servants were worth a total of $600,000, or $20,000,000 in today's currency. This made the Metoyers among the wealthiest people in the U.S., black or white, then or now.[110]

☞ One of the first known American slave owners, if not the first, was a black man named Anthony Johnson. The Virginia slaver from Angola (Africa), who owned both black *and* white slaves, actually helped launch the American slave trade by forcing authorities to legally define the meaning of "slave ownership."[111]

☞ Since American slavery began in the North, it should come as no surprise that thousands of slave plantations once dotted the Northeast, many which, having been obscured for centuries by layers of soil and refuse and the overlay of new structures, are only now being rediscovered, dug up, and examined by archaeologists. This is why, for example, Rhode Island's original—and still official—name, is "Rhode Island and Providence Plantations."[112]

☞ The image of the cruel Southern slave owner beating, starving, and whipping his naked emaciated black slaves is nothing but a ridiculous Yankee myth. Not only was this type of violent psychopathic behavior just as rare in the Old South as it is today, but there were numerous laws that protected black servants, with penalties ranging from fines and imprisonment to actual execution for the most serious offences. Thus the fabled act of "slave abuse" was extremely rare if not completely unknown to most Southerners.[113]

☞ Modern white Americans should not be expected to pay blacks reparations for slavery, for they were not responsible. It was the *Italian* explorer Christopher Columbus who first brought the European version of the institution to the Americas under the auspices of the *Spanish* government.[114]

8

ABOLITION

☛ The American abolition movement began in the South, not in the North. While Northern colonies like Massachusetts were busy expanding the slave trade and legalizing slavery, Southern colonies were busy trying to put a stop to both. Indeed, the very first American colony to attempt abolition was a Southern one: Virginia. Another Southern state, Georgia, was the first to place a prohibition against the importation of slaves into her state constitution.[115]

☛ Among the more famous early Southerners who pushed for abolition were George Washington, Thomas Jefferson, Fernando Fairfax, St. George Tucker, James Madison, Calvin A. Wiley, Reverend James Lyons, Mary and James Chesnut, and Confederate Generals Robert E. Lee, Stonewall Jackson, James Johnston Pettigrew, and Patrick R. Cleburne. General Lee wrote: "There are few, I believe, in this enlightened age, but what will acknowledge that slavery as an institution is a moral and political evil in any country. It is idle to expatiate on its disadvantages. I think it is a greater evil to the white than to the colored race."[116]

☛ Of the 130 abolition societies established before 1827 by Northern abolitionist Benjamin Lundy, over 100, comprising four-fifths of the total membership, were in the South. Early North Carolina, as one example, had a number of well-known "forceful" antislavery leaders, such as Benjamin Sherwood Hedrick and Daniel Reaves Goodlow, and in South Carolina there were the celebrated Quaker sisters Sarah and Angelina Grimké, just a few of the millions of diehard Southern abolitionists.[117]

9

JEFFERSON DAVIS

☛ Because he was a complex private man, Davis has often been misunderstood, leading uninformed pro-North writers to refer to him as "the Sphinx"—that is, one who is cold, inhumane, and aloof. Actually Davis was a warmhearted family man, a social genius, and an intellectual giant, one who was beloved by nearly everyone who ever met him.[118]

☛ Here in the South we have many reasons for admiring our president: Davis was a West Point graduate, a Mexican War hero, a faithful husband, an outstanding father, an eminent Mississippi senator, a bold defender of the Southern Cause, a talented author, and a fearless and knowledgeable protector of the Constitution. Also an honest politician and a brave military man who was popular with his soldiers, Davis was an extraordinary leader of the Confederate nation during what was arguably America's most difficult period. In the eyes of the South these things alone make him a great man, and an immortal hero.[119]

☛ Davis is still called a "traitor" to the U.S. by many in the North. However, since secession was legal (as we proved in Chapter 5), the true traitor was Abraham Lincoln, who trampled over the Constitution, violated the inalienable rights of both the Northern and the Southern people, and committed so many war crimes that the total number has yet to be documented by historians.[120]

☛ Davis is, of course, often politically compared with Lincoln, with the latter routinely trouncing the former among those who belong to the pro-North movement. We in the South take exception to this "final judgement," however, and here is why. Lincoln assured a Yankee victory in great part by subverting the Constitution, engaging in political chicanery (such as rigging elections) and countless war crimes (such as arresting and torturing Northern peace advocates, allowing the theft, abuse, rape and murder of countless Southern civilians), disregarding the Geneva Convention (by sanctioning total war on the South), and psychologically and emotionally manipulating the Northern populace. Davis, on the other hand, helped guarantee Southern defeat by honoring the Confederate Constitution, avoiding political skullduggery, holding his troops to a high standard of behavior, observing the Geneva Convention, discouraging criminal activity among his soldiers, and being honest with the Southern people. Without regard to who won or lost the War, which one then was the superior war president? It is clear where we in the traditional South stand—and why.[121]

☛ When it comes to white racism, Davis is also often compared to Lincoln, always unfavorably in the North. But here are the facts. While Lincoln was blocking emancipation, black enlistment, and black civil rights, and working day and night on his colonization plan to deport all blacks out of the U.S., Davis was busy trying to figure out a way to end Southern slavery, enlist blacks, initiate black civil rights, and incorporate blacks into mainstream American society. In the meantime, during the War, Davis and his wife Varina (Howell) adopted a young black boy, Jim Limber, who they raised as their own in the Confederate White House. The Davises were also widely known as a family who treated their black servants equitably and with great respect, as part of their family in fact. Not surprisingly, President Davis' first Confederate states marshal was a black man. Lincoln never appointed a black man to any position, let alone U.S. states marshal, and unquestionably he would have never adopted a black child. After Lee's surrender, during the Davis family's escape southward, their coachman was a "faithful" free African-American. Later, after the War, the one-time Southern leader and his wife sold their plantation, Brierfield, to a former black servant. Davis even spoke once of a time when he led a unit of "negroes against a lawless body of armed white men . . .," something we can be sure that white separatist Lincoln never did.[122]

☛ The North enjoys criticizing Davis for wanting to continue the War, even after Lee's surrender. However, he had good reason for this. Though Lincoln claimed that "the contest could have been continued indefinitely," this was patently false according to Union General Ulysses S. Grant. In his

1885 *Memoirs*, Grant revealed that if Confederate General Nathan Bedford Forrest's protraction strategy (endorsed by numerous Rebel officers, including General Joseph E. Johnston) had been adopted by the South, the Confederacy would have won the War within one year. (Forrest's plan called for prolonging the conflict—thus exhausting the North—by closing down the Yankees' major supply routes, the Mississippi and Tennessee Rivers). Wrote Grant: "I think that [this] . . . policy was the best one that could have been pursued by the whole South—protract the war, which was all that was necessary to enable them to gain recognition in the end. The North was already growing weary . . . Anything that could have prolonged the war a year beyond the time that it did finally close, would probably have exhausted the North to such an extent that they might then have abandoned the contest and agreed to separation."[123]

☛ Pro-North writers are still assailing the U.S. government for not bringing Davis to trial for "treason," and Davis for "trying to avoid prosecution." Authentic history proves the opposite, however: the U.S. government could not find an attorney to try Davis, while Davis himself repeatedly requested

a trial. In fact, U.S. officials had asked three different prosecuting attorneys to try him, but all three refused, deeming the case thoroughly unwinnable. Why? A public trial would have allowed the South's brilliant legal minds, including Davis', to prove the legality of secession and expose what I call the "Great Yankee Coverup"; that is, the concealment of the many illegalities of Lincoln's War. As one of the North's own lawyers stated: "Gentleman, the Supreme Court of the United States will have to acquit that man under the Constitution when it will be proven to the world that the North waged an unconstitutional warfare against the South." No wonder that before Davis was captured trying to reorganize his armies, President Lincoln and General Grant had ardently "wished and hoped" that he would escape unnoticed into the Southern wilderness.[124]

10

ABRAHAM LINCOLN

☛ We all know Lincoln by his famous nickname "Honest Abe." What many do not realize is that this moniker was bestowed on him as a sarcastic comment on his perfidious behavior, for his dishonest dealings with the American people, not for his alleged "honesty." Thus it would be far more appropriate to call America's sixteenth chief executive "Dishonest Abe,"[125] for he not only lied repeatedly, but he committed a truly dazzling number of well chronicled constitutional, civil, political, ethical, social, religious, spiritual, and moral felonies and misdemeanors.[126]

☛ Here is a highly abbreviated list of just a few of Lincoln's crimes:
- Completely subverting (and perverting) the Constitution.
- Arbitrarily arresting and trying (by military commission) civilian draft resistors and others suspected of "disloyalty."
- Seizing rail and telegraph lines leading to the capital.
- Suppressing and shutting down over 300 hundred pro-peace Northern newspapers, destroying their presses, and arresting their owners.
- Torturing both Northern soldiers (accused of desertion) and Northern citizens (accused of espousing anti-war sentiment); the preferred methods were "violent cold water torture" and being suspended by handcuffed wrists.
- Illegally suspending the writ of *habeas corpus* across the entire U.S., and for the first time in U.S. history.
- Prohibiting the emancipation of slaves by his cabinet members and Union military officers, such as General John. C. Frémont, General David Hunter, John W. Phelps, Jim Lane, and General Simon Cameron (which proves once and for all, if nothing else does, that Lincoln

did not wage war against the South over slavery).
- Unlawfully ordering a naval blockade of Southern ports (unlawful because Lincoln never recognized the Confederacy as a separate nation and war had not yet been declared).
- Declaring all medicines contraband of war (which helped kill countless thousands of Southerners, both soldiers and civilians, not to mention thousands of Yankee soldiers held in Confederate prisons).
- Closing the post office in an effort to prevent anti-Lincoln, anti-war mail from being sent or delivered.
- Refusing to exchange prisoners (which aided in the deaths of thousands of soldiers, both Confederate and Federal).
- Defying the Supreme Court.
- Instituting the largest number of military drafts in U.S. history.
- Shutting down the governments of entire Northern states and arresting members of their state legislatures (usually for suspicion of advocating peace with the South); one of the more notable of these was the state of Maryland, which originally had hoped to join the Confederacy.
- Inaugurating America's first federal monetary monopoly.
- Imprisoning some 38,000 to 50,000 Northern civilians (men, women, and children), without trial, some for as long as four years.
- Incarcerating civilians, like Rebel Vice President Alexander H. Stephens, in military prisons.
- Levying the first personal income tax, launching what would later become the Internal Revenue Service (IRS).
- Preventing governmental debate over secession.
- Ordering the first and only mass execution (and that of his own citizens) by a president in U.S. history.
- Changing the meaning of the "United States" from plural to singular.
- Illegally creating the state of West Virginia from the state of Virginia (Lincoln encouraged the western area of Virginia to secede while he was at war with the South because she had seceded!).
- Rigging Northern elections to skew the outcome in his favor, using such devices as "bayonet votes" (stationing armed Union soldiers at the polls to intimidate voters) and "fictitious states" (inventing states, as mentioned, like West Virginia, in order to accrue more electoral votes).
- Bribing voters, soldiers, and fellow politicians to vote for his party.[127]

☛ Though Lincoln is widely held up today as a "Bible-believing Christian," he was anything but. From his earliest days he was an avowed atheist, skeptic, "infidel," and agnostic, who declared the Bible a fairy tale and rejected the divinity of Christ, even calling him a "bastard." Lincoln never attended church, never belonged to any religion, scoffed at Christian preachers, and once wrote "a little book" proving that the Bible is not the word of God and Jesus is not the Son of God. Lincoln's closest friends and political associates, even his wife Mary, all later testified to the president's atheism and apathy toward, and even hatred of, religion—particularly Christianity.[128]

☛ Though Lincoln was indeed a Republican, the platforms of the two main parties were reversed in the 1860s, making Civil War Republicans liberals and Civil War Democrats conservatives. Thus Lincoln was the 19th-Century's Franklin Delano Roosevelt, Harry Reid, or Barack Hussein Obama, while Jefferson Davis was the 19th-Century's Ronald Reagan, Ron Paul, or Sarah Palin. Ignorance of this fact is what leads to Lincoln worship in both parties today.[129]

☛ Despite his modern day reputation to the contrary, Lincoln never once espoused equal rights for blacks, citizenship for blacks, or black enfranchisement.[130] Instead, as we will see, he spent the first two years of his presidency fighting the idea of emancipation, and finally only relented because he needed the black vote to help get him reelected in 1864, and to replenish the tremendous loss of his white soldiery.[131]

☛ In his spare time, Lincoln—who was voted the worst president in U.S. history by his constituents,[132] and who was an enthusiastic lifelong member of the American Colonization Society (whose stated mission was to rid America of her black population)—vigorously campaigned to have all blacks deported from the U.S. to places such as Africa, South America, and the Caribbean.[133]

11

THE UNION'S NAVAL BLOCKADE

☞ Lincoln's blockade of Southern marine ports, waterways, bays, and inlets was certainly instrumental in aiding the North's victory over the South, the Constitution, and states' rights. However, the blockade was illegal for a variety of reasons, a few which follow.[134]

☞ International law at the time stipulated that for a blockade to be legitimate, every mile of coastline had to be patrolled. Knowing that this was impossible the Union never even attempted it, making this particular military action nothing more than a "paper blockade," and as such, unlawful.[135]

☞ A legal blockade also had to be both 100 percent effective and continuous. Lincoln's was neither. Indeed, the impossibility of barricading every bay, inlet, channel, lagoon, and swamp along the South's 3,550 mile coastline was obvious even to Europeans, who heaped scorn and ridicule upon Lincoln's preposterous plan.[136]

☞ A blockade is also unlawful unless war is formally declared. When Lincoln ordered his blockade on April 19 and 27, 1861, war had not yet been officially announced, either by himself or the U.S. Congress. Lincoln's blockade is just one more reason the War itself was illegal.[137]

12

THE EMANCIPATION PROCLAMATION

☛ Lincoln is called the "Great Emancipator" by his ill-informed devotees. But was he? This chapter will provide the answer.

☛ A careful reading of the Final Emancipation Proclamation (issued January 1, 1863), reveals that it only freed slaves in the South, and even then, only in specific areas of the South. Lincoln's edict purposefully excluded Tennessee, for example (the entire state had been under Yankee control since the fall of Nashville, February 25, 1862), along with numerous Northern-occupied parishes in Louisiana and several counties in Virginia.[138]

☛ The Final Emancipation Proclamation, in fact, was issued only in areas of the South not under Union control. It also did not ban slavery anywhere in the North, where thousands of Yankees still practiced it, including Union officers like General Ulysses S. Grant and his family.[139]

☛ As Lincoln states in the proclamation itself, the North and those places exempted "are for the present left precisely as if this proclamation were not issued." Lincoln could not have made the meaning of this sentence more clear: *slavery was to be allowed to continue in the U.S. (that is, in the North) and in any areas of the South controlled by the U.S. (that is, by the Union armies).* The question Southerners have been asking Northerners for the past century and a half is why, if Lincoln was so interested in black equality, did he only abolish slavery in the South where he had no jurisdiction but not in the

North where he had full control?[140]

☞ The answer is obvious to most Southerners today, just as it was to a majority of them in 1863. If Northerners had asked themselves this same question at the time, they would have never created the myth of Lincoln the "Great Emancipator" in the first place. For in truth, our sixteenth president did not issue the Emancipation Proclamation for the specific purpose of trying to establish black civil rights across the U.S. If that had indeed been his intention he would have also banned slavery in the North and in non-Union occupied areas of the South.[141]

☞ Being the penultimate demagogue, Lincoln had five primary goals in mind when he wrote out the edict, not a single one of them having anything to do with black equality, but everything to do with white needs.[142]

☞ Lincoln revealed the first of these in the proclamation itself by calling it a "war measure," instead of a "civil rights measure." And what a brilliant idea it was. After all, no one could argue against emancipation—not even the most pro-South Northerners, pro-North Southerners, or most bleeding heart liberal Europeans—if Lincoln could prove that freeing the slaves was vital to winning the War.[143]

☞ The second reason Lincoln had for issuing the Emancipation Proclamation was to incite a massive "slave rebellion" in the South, which he hoped would bring about chaos, destabilize Southern society, and destroy her economy. Thus he states in the proclamation that the Yankee government would do nothing to stop any acts that Southern slaves wished to engage in order to attain their freedom.[144]

☞ Unfortunately for Lincoln, like psychopath John Brown's futile attempt at Harper's Ferry to foment black riots in the South, his own nefarious plan came to naught. There was not a single slave rebellion anywhere in the South after he issued the proclamation, as he himself later grudgingly admitted. The truth is that of the South's 3.5 million black servants, 95 percent (nineteen out of twenty) maintained their loyalty to Dixie. Ignoring Lincoln's fake proclamation of "freedom," they instead pledged their allegiance to their home states, to the South, and to their white families. Remaining at home they ran their owner's farms, grew food, produced provisions for the Confederate military, and protected their master's family and property while he was away on the battlefield. And, as we will see, hundreds of thousands donned Confederate grey and fought side-by-side with their Southern white brothers on the battlefield.[145]

☛ The third motivation behind Lincoln's Emancipation Proclamation was to provide manpower for his army and navy, both which, after two years of fighting, were quickly diminishing in numbers due to what I call "The Four D's": desertion, defection, disease, and death. His "military emancipation," as Lincoln himself openly called it, would offset these losses by freeing up the South's 3.5 million slaves, all of whom he assumed would speedily come North and gratefully enlist in the Union military effort. Lincoln himself said as much in a letter to Tennessee's Military Governor Andrew Johnson on March 26, 1863, just three months after issuing the Emancipation Proclamation: "The colored population is the great available and yet unavailed of force for restoring the Union. The bare sight of fifty thousand armed and drilled black soldiers upon the banks of the Mississippi would end the rebellion at once . . ."[146]

☛ Lincoln's assumption that Southern blacks would pour northward and join his armies was an absurd fantasy. This was, in great part, because the president, who consistently and vehemently proclaimed that he was not an abolitionist, did not promise citizenship to blacks—newly freed or already free (and indeed blacks would not become U.S. citizens until 1868, three years after Lincoln's death). Whatever the many reasons for the apathetic response by Southern blacks to his proclamation, between 1863 and 1865 only a small fraction, less than 90,000, of the South's 3.5 million servants ended up in Lincoln's military.[147] As we will see, some 1 million blacks served in the Confederate army, at least five times more than the number of blacks who served in the Union army, a fact one will never find in any pro-North history book on the "Civil War."[148]

☛ The fourth principal reason Lincoln had for issuing the Emancipation Proclamation again had nothing to do with African-American civil rights. The 1864 election was just around the corner and he was desperate to be reelected. But he faced a major problem: since the start of his War he had lost the eleven Confederate states and their eighty-eight electoral votes, along with the support of both anti-war activists and abolitionists. How to accrue additional votes, he asked himself? Again the answer was the Emancipation Proclamation. He would free millions of Southern blacks in the expectation that most would enlist and, as soldiers, would appreciatively cast their votes to reelect him for a second term (he never offered *non-military* blacks the franchise). As we have seen, however, the incumbent president's scheme in this regard was completely unsuccessful.[149]

☛ The fifth and final reason for signing an emancipation proclamation into law concerned Lincoln's lifelong goal, known today by educated blacks as "Abraham Lincoln's white dream": the deportation of all African-Americans out of the country. Lincoln could not even begin this process as long as the South's 3.5 million black servants were considered the "property" of their owners. Emancipation, however, would instantly transform them into "freemen," allowing their legal deportation; or so "Honest Abe" believed. As we will see in the next chapter, this aspect of the Final Emancipation Proclamation also failed, for not only would it have been financially impossible for the U.S. government to pay for the emigration of millions of people, the idiotic bigoted plan had absolutely no support, except for a handful of Lincoln's fellow white supremacists and white separatists. All in all then, from Lincoln's perspective at least, the Emancipation Proclamation was a pathetic blunder. Little more than a transparent and cynical political move, his "war measure" and "military emancipation" did not help gain European support; it did not incite a single slave rebellion in the South; it did not motivate Southern blacks to enlist in his army; it did not inspire Southern blacks to vote for him; and finally, it did not allow him to launch his nationwide black deportation program. The fact that it technically and actually freed no slaves did not trouble Lincoln in the least, as this was never the intention of his proclamation to begin with.[150]

☛ There are still numerous other reasons Lincoln should not be considered the "Great Emancipator." For one thing, he had to be cajoled, harassed, and finally pushed (by abolition leaders such as Horace Greeley and Frederick Douglass) into even considering abolition, which is the main reason it took him two years to issue the Final Emancipation Proclamation. If the War had been about slavery, why did he not issue it the first week he was in office? And furthermore, if the War had been over slavery, why did it continue for another two years *after* he issued it?[151]

☛ Little wonder that the Richmond *Examiner* called the Emancipation proclamation the most shocking crime perpetuated by a politician in U.S. history, or that English newspapers, like the London *Times* called it a tragic document, or that the London *Spectator* termed it a deceitful fabrication. And what rank hypocrisy it was, for at the time not only was slavery still alive and well in the North, but free Northern blacks were still not allowed to vote, sit on juries, attend white churches, be buried in white cemeteries, marry whites, or even become U.S. citizens.[152]

☛ Since Lincoln was not concerned with black civil rights, he was also prepared to allow the Southern states to take all the time they needed to abolish slavery, as he stated, at least until the year 1900 or even longer if need be.[153]

☛ Lincoln did not even plan on making abolition in the South permanent. On February 3, 1865, at the Hampton Roads Peace Conference (just two months before the end of the War), according to those present, Lincoln's "own opinion was, that as the Proclamation was a *war measure*, and would have effect only from its being an exercise of the war power, as soon as the war ceased, it would be inoperative for the future. It would be held to apply only to such slaves as had come under its operation while it was in active exercise. This was his individual opinion."[154]

☛ In the beginning Lincoln was even willing to sign the 1861 Corwin Amendment to the Constitution, which would have allowed slavery to continue in perpetuity without any interference from the national government. Dishonest Abe was clearly not the "Great Emancipator"![155]

13

LINCOLN'S BLACK COLONIZATION PLAN

☛ Though it is unfamiliar to the public because pro-North historians have so vigorously suppressed the fact, it is well-known in the South that Lincoln had a lifelong association with the American Colonization Society (ACS), a popular Yankee organization founded in 1816 in Washington, D.C., by a Northerner, New Jerseyan Reverend Robert Finley. The primary mission of the ACS was to create an all-white, black-free America by deporting ("colonizing") as many African-Americans as possible, and as quickly as possible.[156]

☛ Not only was Lincoln an enthusiastic supporter and member of the ACS, at one time he even served as an ACS chapter leader in Illinois, a state whose legislature he personally convinced to finance the deportation of free blacks.[157]

☛ Though much of the proof of Lincoln's ties to the ACS have been destroyed or concealed, there is still evidence to be found. During his famous February 27, 1860, Cooper Union speech in New York, for example, the soon-to-be Republican (then liberal) presidential nominee brought up, as he so often did, the topic of colonization, hoping to make new converts. Quoting Thomas Jefferson's autobiography, Lincoln said hopefully: "In the language of Mr. Jefferson, uttered many years ago, 'It is still in our power to direct the process of emancipation, and deportation, peaceably, and in such slow degrees, as that the evil will wear off insensibly;

and their places be . . . filled up by free white laborers.'" In other words, for white supremacist Lincoln—who often referred to blacks as "niggers" and "an inferior race"—black deportation achieved two goals simultaneously: it would rid the U.S. of the "evil" presence of blacks and eliminate the threat of blacks taking jobs away from whites.[158]

☛ So adamant was Lincoln about expatriating American blacks that he was willing to settle them almost anyplace—as long as it was, as he said, "without the United States." This included Europe, Latin America, or the Caribbean, or anywhere else they would be accepted. As such, he funded experimental black colonies in what are now Panama and Belize, as well as in Haiti. But he seemed to have a special interest in the African colony of Liberia. Indeed, Africa was always his first choice. He would even pay the resettlement costs of any and all African-Americans willing to volunteer to be shipped out of the U.S. The more the better, in his opinion. Here is what our racist sixteenth president said about black slavery and black colonization on October 16, 1854, during a speech at Peoria, Illinois: "If all earthly power were given me, I should not know what to do as to the existing institution. My first impulse would be to free all the slaves, and send them to Liberia—to their own native land."[159]

☛ If his deportation plan turned out to be unworkable, Lincoln had another one nearly as good, or so he believed: corral American blacks in their own all-black state, preferably one far from his own home state of Illinois. This idea, yet another one of his many harebrained prejudiced notions, was presented by Lincoln to the public on September 15, 1858, at one of his famous debates with Senator Stephen A. Douglas.[160]

☛ Lincoln's true feelings about blacks were never in doubt at the time. Just two months earlier, on July 17, 1858, for instance, Old Abe told an equally bigoted audience at Springfield, Illinois: "What I would most desire would be the separation of the white and black races."[161]

☛ Pro-North writers like to play down Lincoln's racism, as well as his devotion to black colonization, pretending that it all completely disappeared by the time he became president in March 1861. The truth, however, is that his desire to racially "cleanse" American soil of the black man actually grew stronger over time. One need only look at a few of his presidential speeches.

☛ As he did whenever the opportunity arose, *President* Lincoln used his First Annual Message to Congress on December 3, 1861, for instance, to promote the idea of deporting blacks, in this case, free blacks: "It might be well to consider, too," he declared, "whether the free colored people already in the United States could not, so far as individuals may desire, be included in such colonization." As a result of this speech, in 1861 and 1862 the U.S. Congress had $600,000 (about $15 million in today's currency) set aside to aid in Lincoln's colonization plan to send as many free blacks as possible out of the country.[162]

☛ On September 22, 1862—just four months before issuing the Final Emancipation Proclamation—he issued the Preliminary Emancipation Proclamation, which contained the following remarkable statement: "It is my purpose . . . to again recommend . . . that the effort to colonize [that is, deport] persons of African descent with their consent upon this continent or elsewhere . . . will be continued." Why did this sensational clause, directed at the U.S. Congress, not make it into the Final Emancipation Proclamation, issued only a few months later on January 1, 1863? Against his wishes Lincoln's own cabinet members talked him out of including it because it might further alienate abolitionists, a group that was already bitterly disappointed with Lincoln's refusal to abolish slavery after being in the White House for over two years. Lincoln would need their votes in his upcoming bid for reelection in 1864. Promising to deport newly freed blacks was hardly the way to win the hearts, minds, and votes of abolitionists. And so the item on black colonization, one of Lincoln's most ardent lifelong aspirations, was struck from the Final Emancipation Proclamation. Thus this version, the only one known by the public today, is not the Emancipation Proclamation Lincoln wanted. It is the one forced on him by his cabinet and by political expediency.[163]

☛ Shortly thereafter, however, just one month before issuing the Final Emancipation Proclamation, he reemphasized his position on the issue, lest anyone should forget. In his Second Annual Message to Congress on December 1, 1862, *President* Lincoln stated unambiguously: "I cannot make it better known than it already is, that I strongly favor colonization."[164]

☛ In this same speech Lincoln once again asked Congress to set aside funding for black deportation, and even suggested adding an amendment to the Constitution to expedite it. According to Lincoln: "Congress may appropriate money and otherwise provide for colonizing free colored persons, with their own consent, at any place or places without the United States."[165]

☛ When President Lincoln's adherence to the ACS mission is pointed out to pro-North historians, they always counter by stating that "he rejected the ACS before his death." This turns out to be yet another Yankee myth, however. The truth is that Lincoln never abandoned his obsession with exiling all blacks from the U.S. In fact, he lobbied feverishly for colonization right up to the day he died, two years after issuing the Emancipation Proclamation, as Yankee General Benjamin "the Beast" Butler attests. According to Butler, in March 1865, just one month before Lincoln was assassinated by Northerner John Wilkes Booth, the president called the general to the White House to discuss the practicalities of black expatriation.[166]

☛ Emancipation first. Colonization second. This was Lincoln's plan for blacks from the beginning to the very end of his life. Had he survived John Wilkes Booth's attack, there is no question that he would have done everything in his power to fulfill the second half of his program. Thus it was, in great part, Booth who finally freed American blacks, not Abraham Lincoln. For the stark reality is that African-Americans, whether enslaved or free, would have never been completely liberated while Lincoln was alive—and indeed they were not. Booth's bullet was the true "Great Emancipator."[167]

☛ During an 1859 speech at Cincinnati, Ohio, Lincoln summed up his lifelong feelings on the races this way: "If there was a necessary conflict between the white man and the negro, I should be for the white man."[168]

14

BLACKS & THE CONFEDERACY

☛ Our error-filled pro-North history books teach that blacks would not and did not defend the Southern Confederacy. But they are wrong. In fact, more blacks fought in the Confederate armies than fought in the Union armies. The Union possessed about 3 million soldiers. Of these about 200,000 were black, 6 percent of the total. The Confederacy had about 1 million soldiers. Of these an estimated 300,000 were black, 30 percent of the total—24 percent more than fought for Lincoln.[169]

☛ And these numbers are conservative if we use the definition of a "private soldier" as determined by the German-American Union General August Valentine Kautz in 1864: "In the fullest sense, any man in the military service who receives pay, whether sworn in or not, is a soldier, because he is subject to military law. Under this general head, laborers, teamsters, sutlers, chaplains, etc., are soldiers." Using Kautz's definition of a "private soldier," some 2 million Southerners fought in the Confederacy: 1 million whites and perhaps as many as 1 million blacks. As most of the 4 million blacks (3.5 million servants, 500,000 free) living in the South at the time of Lincoln's War remained loyal to Confederacy, and as at least 500,000 to 1 million of these either worked in or fought in the Rebel army and navy in some capacity, Kautz' definition raises the percentage of Southern blacks who defended the Confederacy as real soldiers to as much as 50 percent of the total Confederate soldier population.[170] That is five times, or 500 percent, more than served in the Union military.[171]

☛ There were so many black Rebels on the battlefield that Northern soldiers, most who were overtly racist, were completely dumbstruck at the sight. And their fear was justified: Confederate blacks were known to be ferocious fighters, fearless soldiers, and crack shots. Indeed, the first Northerner killed in the War, Major Theodore Winthrop of the 7th Regiment, New York State Militia, was brought down by a black Confederate sharpshooter at the Battle of Bethel Church, June 10, 1861.[172]

☛ General Stonewall Jackson's army alone contained some 3,000 black soldiers. Clad "in all kinds of uniforms," and armed with "rifles, muskets, sabres, bowie-knives, dirks, etc.," to the shocked Yankee soldiers they were "manifestly an integral portion of the Southern Confederacy." On March 1, 1865, Yankee Colonel John G. Parkhurst sent a battlefield dispatch to General William D. Whipple, reporting that: "The rebel authorities are enrolling negroes in Mississippi preparatory to putting them into service."[173]

☛ If more proof of Southern black support for the Confederacy is needed we need look no further than a letter written by former *Northern* slave Frederick Douglass to Lincoln in 1862. In it the black civil rights leader uses the example of the overwhelming number of blacks in the Confederate army to urge the president to allow blacks to officially enlist in the Union army (Lincoln had steadfastly refused up until that time). Wrote Douglass to the bigoted chief executive: "There are at the present moment, many colored men in the Confederate Army doing duty not only as cooks, servants and laborers, but as real soldiers, having muskets on their shoulders and bullets in their pockets, ready to shoot down loyal [Yankee] troops, and do all that soldiers may do to destroy the Federal government and build up that of the traitors and rebels. There were such soldiers at Manassas, and they are probably there still. There is a negro in the [Confederate] army as well as in the fence, and our Government is likely to find it out before the war comes to an end. That the negroes are numerous in the rebel army, and do for that army it heaviest work, is beyond question." Unfortunately, the reality of the black Confederate soldier does not conform to Northern and New South myths about Southern blacks and slavery, and so it has been disregarded and suppressed. But we are bringing it back into the light.[174]

☛ After Lincoln issued his fake and illegal Emancipation Proclamation, Southern historical studies reveal that only 5 percent or less left Dixie for the North. A full 95 percent of the South's black servants remained right where they were after so-called "emancipation," preferring to stay with their families and friends on the land of their birth, on the farms and plantations they loved, near the graves of their time-honored ancestors.[175]

☛ Even Lincoln recognized the immense contribution of Southern black soldiers to the Confederacy, as he stated on March 17, 1865: "There is one thing about *the negro's fighting for the rebels* which we can know as well as they can, and that is that they cannot at the same time *fight in their armies* and stay at home and make bread for them."[176]

☛ Blacks were far from being the only minority to serve in the Confederate military. Actually, like Southern society itself at the time, as now, the Rebel army was a highly multiracial, multicultural group comprised of every race and dozens of different nationalities. Though—thanks to the vicious Yankee custom of burning down Southern courthouses—exact statistics are impossible to come by, we Southern historians have determined that the following numbers are roughly accurate. In descending numerical order the Confederate army and navy was composed of about 1 million European-Americans, 300,000 to 1 million African-Americans, 70,000 Native-Americans (a band who is shown on the cover of this book), 60,000 Latin-Americans, 50,000 foreigners, 12,000 Jewish-Americans, and 10,000 Asian-Americans. True Southerners, of all races, continue to be proud of our region's multiracial history, and of the many contributions made to Dixie by individuals of all colors, creeds, and nationalities.[177]

15

BLACKS & THE UNION

☞ While Lincoln was thinking up ways to delay and even avoid black enlistment in the Union armies, the Confederacy was busy signing up African-Americans as fast as possible. Southern black enlistment came even before the War's first major conflict, the Battle of First Manassas (First Bull Run to Yanks) on July 18, 1861. In June 1861, one year and three months before the Union officially sanctioned the recruitment of blacks in August 1862, and almost two years before Lincoln began arming blacks in March 1863, the Tennessee legislature passed a statute allowing Confederate Governor Isham G. Harris to receive into military service "all male free persons of color, between the ages of 15 and 50."[178]

☞ On February 4, 1862, the Virginia legislature passed a bill to enroll all of the state's free Negroes for service in the Confederate army. Earlier, on November 23, 1861, a seven-mile long line of Confederate soldiers was marched through the streets of New Orleans. Among them was a regiment of 1,400 free black volunteers. Hundreds of other such examples could be given. We have already seen that perhaps as many as 80 percent more blacks fought for the Confederacy than for the Union. Anti-South proponents have carefully suppressed such facts, making our already Northern-slanted history books even more incomplete, inaccurate, and misleading than they were to begin with.[179]

☞ Yankee history books teach that the Union formed all-black troops before the Confederacy did, but again this turns out to be nothing more than false anti-South propaganda. The South's first all-black militia was officially organized on April 23, 1861, only nine days after the first battle of the War at Fort Sumter, South Carolina. The unit, known as the "Native Guards (colored)," was "duly and legally enrolled as a part of the militia of the State, its officers being commissioned by Thomas O. Moore, Governor and Commander-in-Chief of the State of Louisiana . . ." In contrast, the North's first all-black militia, the First South Carolina Volunteers, was not commissioned until over a year and a half later (on November 7, 1862), under Yankee Colonel Thomas Wentworth Higginson.[180]

☛ We have long been taught that while the South was racist toward her black soldiers, the North was not. This is obviously erroneous since, as Tocqueville and dozens of other early travelers pointed out, white racism was far more severe in the North. Indeed, white Yankee soldiers were well-known for their racial bigotry and utter intolerance of blacks. This is just one of the many reasons Lincoln would not permit blacks to serve as active combatants in the U.S. military during the first half of his War. Lincoln's hesitation was certainly warranted, but not for the reason he claimed (that blacks would lose their weapons, etc.): when he finally allowed full-fledged black recruitment, white soldiers hissed and booed, desertions increased, and a general "demoralization" set in across the entire Federal military.[181]

☛ The mere mention of the idea of "black enlistment" brought many white regiments close to insurrection. A Yankee soldier with the 90th Illinois reported on the general feeling among his fellow Union compatriots at the time: "Not one of our boys wants to give guns to the Negroes. This is a white man's war and that's the way we want to keep it. Besides we have no desire to fight next to blacks on the battlefield," he asserted.[182]

☛ Northern white outrage at the idea of enlisting blacks was somewhat mitigated when Lincoln ordered the army and navy to be racially segregated (in contrast, Confederate troops were racially integrated). But newly recruited blacks were not happy with the president's command that all colored troops were to be officered by whites. Even pro-North historians have had to concede that most white Northern soldiers were "bitterly hostile . . . to Negro troops."[183]

☛ White Yankee racism continued well into the War. During inclement weather, for example, white Yankee soldiers were known to beat black Yankee soldiers, then push them out into the freezing night air in order to have the tents all to themselves.[184]

☛ Most white Union officers never completely accepted commanding black troops, as there was "no prestige" in it. In fact so few white officers could be found who were willing to "lower" themselves to leading blacks that white privates, induced with the promise of promotion, finally had to be virtually coerced into taking the positions. The situation got so out of hand that Federal officers had to be ordered to "treat black soldiers as soldiers," and the "n" word, along with degrading disciplinary action and routine offensive language aimed at blacks, had to be banned with harsh punishments. Meanwhile white Union soldiers continued to put on minstrel shows that satirized and humiliated African-Americans, a not uncommon form of entertainment, particularly on Yankee warships.[185]

☛ But Northern white racism in the U.S. army often manifested in far more serious and diabolical ways. Southern diaries, letters, and journals are replete with reports of incredible Yankee brutality against not only white Southern women they came across, but black Southern women as well, even against those that had at first cheered them on as liberators. Yankee soldiers' crimes against black females included robbery, pillage, beatings, torture, rape, and even murder. Southern black males were often treated even worse by their Northern "emancipators." Those who survived such crimes were taken, against their will at gunpoint, from their relatively peaceful, healthy, and safe lives of service and domesticity on the plantation, to the filth, hardships, and dangers of life on the battlefield, where at least 50 percent of them died alone in muddy ditches fighting for the Yanks against their own native land: the South.[186]

☛ Those blacks who resisted "involuntary enlistment" into Lincoln's army were sometimes shot or bayoneted on the spot. When black soldiers rebelled against the abuse of white Yankee soldiers, they were whipped. Both white and black Union soldiers were known to abuse Southern slaves who remained loyal to Dixie, entering their homes, shooting bullets through the walls, overturning furniture, and stealing various personal items. Is any of this shocking? Not when we realize that this was all merely a continuation of Lincoln's policy of coercion, the same one he had used to invade the

South in an attempt to destroy states' rights in the first place.[187]

☛ Newly "freed" black males were routinely used as Yankee shock troops, sent first into battle in conflicts usually known beforehand to be hopeless, where they would draw fire and take the brunt of the violence, sparing the lives of Northern whites. This is almost certainly what Lincoln was intimating in his letter to James C. Conkling on August 26, 1863, when he wrote: ". . . whatever negroes can be got to do as soldiers, leaves just so much less for white soldiers to do in saving the Union." This included, of course, receiving cold Confederate steel.[188]

☛ Blacks who were finally allowed to enlist in the Union army by their reluctant president, however, were in for a rude surprise if they expected to don a fancy new blue uniform and fight next to whites on the battlefield. For at the beginning of black enlistment, Lincoln turned nearly all freed black males into common workers who performed what can only be described as "forced labor"; in other words, slavery. Their work, in fact, was identical to the drudgery they had experienced as slaves. Black military duties under Lincoln included construction, serving officers (known in the South as "body servants"), cooking, washing clothes and dishes, tending livestock, and cleaning stables.[189]

☛ Actually, the first black soldiers in the U.S. military were not allowed to serve as active combatants in any form; rather they were signed up specifically to work as ordinary grunts: teamsters, blacksmiths, carpenters, masons, scouts, longshoremen, pioneers, wheelwrights, medical assistants, orderlies, laundry workers, spies, and of course, "slaves," almost anything but armed fighters. Most were to be used merely for monotonous guard duty, or as Lincoln put it in his Final Emancipation Proclamation, "to garrison forts, positions, stations, and other places, and to man vessels of all sorts in said service."[190]

☛ This so-called "Freedmen's labor system," authorized by Lincoln and overseen by Yankee General Nathaniel Prentiss Banks, was so blatantly racist that Banks was even roundly criticized by other Northerners, who accused him of "forcing blacks back into slavery." The brutal U.S. government program was also rife with corruption and fraud: freed blacks were regularly whipped while their already paltry wages were often "withheld" by unscrupulous and inhumane white Northerners who pocketed the money then disappeared.[191]

☛ Lincoln's own personal racism toward his black soldiers seemed boundless. Along with the bigoted policies already mentioned, he also refused to grant Northern black soldiers equal treatment in any way. For example, he gave his black soldiers half the pay of white soldiers: white U.S. privates were paid thirteen dollars per month, while black U.S. privates were paid just seven dollars per month. Contrast this with the Confederacy: in some Southern states blacks were actually paid up to three times the rate of whites for military service. Three of the seven dollars of the black Union soldiers' monthly pay was a deduction for clothing, a deduction not imposed on white Union soldiers. Often even this small amount was withheld from black recruits by Yank officers, who sometimes simply "skimmed" the money for themselves, only one of dozens of ways the U.S. defrauded African-Americans during the War. Lincoln also refused to give black soldiers bonuses, pensions, or support for dependents, all which were regularly accorded to white soldiers. He would not even allow black soldiers equal medical treatment. Medicines and emergency care were to go to whites first, blacks second.[192]

☛ It is obvious that even after reluctantly allowing blacks into the Union army and navy, Lincoln and his military men continued to see them as little more than servile laborers and cannon-fodder.[193]

16

CIVIL WAR PRISONS

☛ If we are to believe the fairy tales of pro-North historians, the Confederacy was needlessly cruel to Union prisoners, particularly at places like Georgia's Andersonville Prison, where nearly 13,000 Federal inmates died "unnecessarily." The truth is that those in charge of Confederate prisons were not sadistic psychopaths. They did their best under horrible conditions. What Yankee myth does not teach you is the fact that these conditions were made worse by the North during a war that the North herself started![194]

☛ On July 22, 1862, for example, a cartel was ratified by both sides for the mutual exchange of all prisoners. Had this agreement been honored throughout the conflict, horrors like the Confederacy's Andersonville Prison would not have occurred. Unfortunately for the 12,912 Union prisoners who perished at Andersonville, along with thousands in other Confederate prisons, the Yankees broke the cartel on April 17, 1863. It was on this date that Lincoln's Secretary of War Edwin M. Stanton and General Ulysses S. Grant, foolishly believing that the Union-Confederate prisoner exchange was benefitting the South and hurting the North, ordered a halt to the program. The results of this unethical action were inevitable. Southern prisons quickly became overcrowded, with all of the attendant ills of any overpopulated city: dirt, infections, illness and disease, lack of food and clothing, scarcity of medicines, and increased violence and death.[195]

☛ Stanton and Grant were only partially responsible for this nightmare, however. Lincoln must also be held accountable, for it was he who, as commander-in-chief, sanctioned their order to break the prison exchange cartel. Lincoln was responsible in other ways as well. His heartless and illegal blockade of Southern ports, for instance, virtually stopped the import of medical supplies, such as life saving medicines, bandages, pain killers, and surgical equipment.[196]

☛ The situation both North and South became so awful that even soulless Lincoln and stone-hearted Grant were forced to recognize the cruelty and stupidity of their actions. While Lincoln refused to end his unlawful blockade, in February 1865 (now knowing the Union would be victorious) he did terminate Grant's order to halt the exchange of prisoners, at which time he began allowing the transfer of sick inmates. Lamentably, this came too late in the conflict: thousands were already dead or permanently disabled.[197]

☛ For Southerners one of the most heartrending consequences of Andersonville was the Yankee court-martial, shameful trial (in which Northern "eyewitnesses" openly lied in court), and illegal execution of the prison camp's commandant, Confederate Major Henry Wirz. Anti-South crusaders, who still refer to him as "the fiend," will never acknowledge what all true Southerners know: under the worst circumstances imaginable, the Swiss-American Wirz had not only not committed any crimes, he had done an amazing job (prison rations were the same, for example, as Rebel soldiers in the field) under horrendous circumstances. Thus in the South Wirz will always be considered a hero, a victim of Yankee incompetence and ruthlessness, and a whipping boy for the Yank's lust for retribution.[198]

☛ The reality is that most of the suffering took place in Yankee prisons. As just one example, some 6,000 Confederate prisoners were tortured then purposefully starved to death at Chicago's notorious Camp Douglas, a place rightly known as "Eighty Acres of Hell." The real truth about Civil War prison systems came from Lincoln's own Secretary of War Stanton, who noted that a higher percentage of Southern POWs perished in Yankee prisons than Northern POWs in Confederate prisons. Some estimate the Rebel prisoner loss to be as high as 200,000, while the Yankee prisoner loss was closer to between 23,000 and 30,000.[199] Southern Truth.

17

THE KU KLUX KLAN

☞ To this day the pro-North movement preaches that the Ku Klux Klan of the Civil War era was a racist and violent organization with only one purpose: to drive blacks from America. As we have seen, however, this was actually the goal of Lincoln's favorite organization, the Yankee-founded group known as the American Colonization Society, at one time headed by Dishonest Abe's lifelong political idol, slave owner Henry Clay.[200]

☞ In reality the KKK of the Old South was an anti-Yankee organization, one that quite correctly described itself as an institution of "chivalry, humanity, mercy, and patriotism." In fact, during the first two years of its existence this noble social aid organization was comprised of thousands of white and black members, for its sole mission was to protect and care for the weak, the disenfranchised, and the innocent, whatever their race. This explains why there was an all-black Ku Klux Klan that operated for several years in the Nashville area.[201]

☞ The KKK's other primary goal was to help maintain law and order across the South. Though Lincoln's Reconstruction program had called for military rule, its implementation had the opposite effect. Lawlessness and vicious criminal behavior became commonplace, problems exacerbated by the appearance of thick-skinned, greedy carpetbaggers (Northerners) and treasonous, unscrupulous scallywags (Northernized Southerners), both groups which sought to prey on and exploit the long-suffering Southern survivors of Lincoln's War.[202]

☞ Proof of this is that when carpetbag rule ended in 1869, this, the original

KKK, immediately came to an end as well all across the "Invisible Empire" (that is, the Southern states). For when Southerners were allowed to begin to take back political control of their own states, there was no longer any need for a self-protective social welfare organization like the KKK. This is why former Confederate officer and Southern hero General Nathan Bedford Forrest, the Klan's most famous and influential supporter, called in its members and shut the entire fraternity down in March of that year. By the end of 1871 the KKK had disappeared from most areas of the South. Still, now inaccurately associated with bigotry, the damage had been done, and to this day the original Reconstruction KKK has been branded, unfairly and unhistorically, with the "racist" label.[203]

☞ It should be noted here for the record that the KKK of today, which emerged in the 1920s, is in no way similar or even connected to the original KKK of the Southern postbellum period, which lasted a mere three years and four months: December 1865 to March 1869. Indeed, there are indications that the modern KKK is far more popular outside the South, with flourishing clans in Indiana, New York, California, Oregon, and Connecticut, just to name a few. Illinois in particular, Lincoln's adopted home state, has also seen a recent resurgence of Klan activity.[204]

☞ The Civil War KKK was not purely Southern, for it borrowed many of its traditions and rituals from pre-KKK Northern groups, such as the Order of the Star Spangled Banner, founded in Boston in 1849.[205]

☞ Rebel General Nathan Bedford Forrest has long been branded with being both the founder and the first grand wizard of the KKK, more Yankee falsehoods. The names of the six men who started the KKK on Christmas Eve 1865 in a haunted house in Pulaski, Tennessee, are well-known: J. Calvin Jones, Captain John C. Lester, Richard R. Reed, Captain James R. Crowe, Frank O. McCord, and Captain John B. Kennedy. Forrest did not begin to associate with the organization until two years later, in 1867. Obviously then he could not have been either its founder or its first leader. As mentioned, he did, however, close down the group, an act for which the pro-North movement has, as expected, never given him credit.[206]

18

THE CONFEDERATE FLAG

☛ The Confederate Battle Flag, with its striking blue cross, thirteen white stars, and bright red field, has become the anti-South movement's favorite weapon against Dixie. Forever condemned as a symbol of Southern white racism and white supremacy, South-hating advocates use the flag to continue the Yankee and liberal effort to demonize, humiliate, and degrade the South. But is this effort justified? Of course not! Just because a flag, or any other object, is used by a racist hate group does not automatically give it the same meaning to everyone else. If this were true then the U.S. flag would also have to be denounced, for numerous modern day hate groups used it as their sole organizational symbol.[207]

☛ Here are the facts about the Confederate Battle Flag: designed by South Carolinian William Porcher Miles (patterned after his state's secession flag), it is a symbol of Southern heritage, a heritage that includes all races. For not only did all races help settle and build the South, all races also fought against the Yankees under the Confederate Battle Flag. We will recall that the Confederate military was comprised of 1 million European-Americans, 300,000 to as many as 1 million African-Americans, 70,000 Native-Americans, 60,000 Latin-Americans, 50,000 foreigners, 12,000 Jewish-Americans, and 10,000 Asian-Americans. These statistics prove to the world like nothing else can, that from the beginning the Confederacy was a multiracial, multicultural society, one that fought, not to oppress the black race or any other race, but for the constitutional rights and personal freedom of all her people. Those who say anything different are either lying or are ignorant of genuine Southern history, plain and simple.[208]

☛ Contrary to popular thought, the South is not a "white region," and never was. Indeed, Dixie is the unique and special place it is today because of the culinary, architectural, sartorial, political, social, artistic, musical, and literary contributions made by all the races. If one section of the U.S. had to be called a melting pot of multiracial influences, it would be the South, not the North.[209]

☛ The Confederate Battle Flag then turns out to be anything but a symbol of white racism or white supremacy. Those who created it never intended it to have this meaning, and those who fought under it never thought of it as having this meaning. The descendants of those soldiers today have also never perceived it in this way, as both myself and many living black Confederates can testify.[210]

☛ If anything it would be more accurate to call our flag a symbol of racial inclusiveness and multiculturalism, one founded on the Christian principles extolled by Jesus, whose main tenants were love and universal brotherhood.[211] For the Confederate Battle Flag was designed around the Christian crosses of Great Britain's flag (Saint George's Cross), Scotland's flag (Saint Andrew's Cross), and Ireland's flag (Saint Patrick's Cross).[212]

☛ In summary, our Battle Flag, the beautiful Southern Cross, is an emblem of American patriotism, strict constitutionalism, Christian love, and Southern heritage. As such, it is a flag that all Southerners, and all lovers of liberty, should display with pride and honor whenever and wherever possible. Conservative Southern Founding Father, Thomas Jefferson, the "Father of the Declaration of Independence," would heartily approve.[213]

19

RECONSTRUCTION

☛ Lincoln and his cronies invented the word "Reconstruction" as part of their anti-South, pro-North propaganda campaign to hide the truth about the War from the public, as well as forever tarnish the South's reputation and honor. In fact, it was little more than a great whitewash of American history, for no true rebuilding of the Southern states was intended, and indeed none ever took place during the twelve Reconstruction years, 1865 to 1877. What did take place was an attempt at the deconstruction of the Old South and its replacement by the "New South," for one of Lincoln's stated goals was always to Northernize the South and recreate it in the image of the North. This was to occur primarily through massive industrialization and the wholesale takeover of homes, plantations, businesses, and even entire towns, by Yankee investors, and more perniciously, the takeover of Southern schools by Yankee teachers and Southern state governments by Yankee politicians.[214]

☛ Since, naturally, the agrarian South would not go down this road willingly, she had to be coerced, which is exactly what the North proceeded to do the very day Lee laid down his arms at Appomattox. But turning the South into a military state under the rule of despotic and often corrupt, arrogant, and violent Yankee officers, did nothing to engender warm feelings toward the North. At the same time, in an attempt to thoroughly "Unionize" Southerners, Confederate flags and uniforms were banned, former Confederate officers were required to pay exorbitant taxes and barred from holding political office, and former white Confederates were prohibited from voting while illiterate blacks were given the franchise.[215]

☛ Worse, the North's Reconstruction soldiers often harassed Dixie's citizens, ousted her families from their farms, pillaged their homes, robbed their men, and raped their women. Sadistically, many Southerners were even put on racks and tortured with thumbscrews. Why? What could possibly justify such acts? What did any of this madness have to do with either preserving the Union or abolishing slavery, the alleged reasons Lincoln went to War? Only the Yankees who committed these crimes know the answer.[216]

☛ Southerners responded to the violent insanity of carpetbag-scallywag rule just as they did to the North's first illegal invasion of their homeland in 1861: they "rebelled" a second time, and with the help of a new and more enlightened president, Rutherford B. Hayes, by 1877 they were able to drive the last hated Yankee soldiers out of the South. Free at last from the iron fist of Yankee dictatorship, Southern families returned to their homes and reopened their shops and schools (what was left of them). Former Confederate officers were quickly voted into office and the Confederate Flag was proudly flown once again outside every house, farm, and storefront. With Dixie now in tatters, Southerners did their level best to pick up where they had left off before Lincoln's illegal invasion twelve years earlier.[217]

☛ In the end, like the "Civil War" itself, Reconstruction was an utter failure, doomed by the impossibility of its very mission: to make the leisurely, religious, agricultural, conservative South into an exact duplicate of the fast-paced, atheistic, industrialized, liberal North. Victorian traditional Southerners were not about to let this happen. Even many carpet-baggers themselves realized the futility of trying to Northernize Dixie, correctly calling it "a fool's errand." One of these, Ohio carpetbagger Albion W. Tourgee, put it this way: "The North and the South are simply convenient names for two distinct, hostile, and irreconcilable ideas,—two civilizations they are sometimes called, especially at the South. At the North there is somewhat more of intellectual arrogance; and we are apt to speak of the one as civilization, and of the other as a species of barbarism. These two must always be in conflict until the one prevails, and the other falls. To uproot the one, and plant the other in its stead, is not the work of a moment or a day. That was our mistake. We [Yankees] tried to superimpose the civilization, the idea of the North, upon the South at a moment's warning. We presumed, that, by the suppression of rebellion, the Southern white man had become identical with the Caucasian of the

North in thought and sentiment; and that the slave, by emancipation, had become a saint and a Solomon at once. So we tried to build up communities there which should be identical in thought, sentiment, growth, and development, with those of the North. It was a fool's errand."[218]

☛ Indeed, "Reconstruction" only rubbed salt into an already open and festering wound created at the Mason-Dixon Line by Lincoln and his dictatorial administration. And few children of Dixie epitomized the Southern revulsion toward Yankeedom more than Edmund Ruffin, Virginian, farmer, agricultural reformer, and worshiper of the Old South and her traditions. After being conquered and humiliated for four years during Lincoln's War, he loaded up his shotgun and made one last entry in his diary. The date was June 17, 1865. "Reconstruction" had already begun: "I here declare my unmitigated hatred to Yankee rule—to all political, social and business connections with the Yankees and to the Yankee race. Would that I could impress these sentiments, in their full force, on every living Southerner and bequeath them to every one yet to be born! May such sentiments be held universally in the outraged and down-trodden South, though in silence and stillness, until the now far-distant day shall arrive for just retribution for Yankee usurpation, oppression and atrocious outrages, and for deliverance and vengeance for the now ruined, subjugated and enslaved Southern States! . . . And now with my latest writing and utterance, and with what will be near my latest breath, I here repeat and would willingly proclaim my unmitigated hatred to Yankee rule—to all political, social and business connections with Yankees, and the perfidious, malignant and vile Yankee race."[219]

☛ Unfortunately, Lincoln's left wing liberal dream (to Northernize the South) is still very much alive. Now aided by thousands of disloyal "New South" scallywags, the sinister process to eliminate all Southernness from Dixie continues, stronger now than ever before. At every opportunity true Southerners continue to resist the trend to exterminate Southern society. To those who are committed to Northernizing us, we say: heed the words of Mr. Tourgee!

NOTES

1 Seabrook, EYWTATCWIW, p. 13.
2 For more on this topic, see Seabrook, AL, passim; Seabrook, L, passim; Seabrook, TAHSR, passim; Seabrook, ARB, passim.
3 Seabrook, EYWTATCWIW, pp. 23-24.
4 Seabrook, EYWTATCWIW, pp. 13, 24.
5 Seabrook, EYWTATCWIW, p. 24.
6 Seabrook, EYWTATCWIW, p. 25.
7 Seabrook, EYWTATCWIW, p. 25.
8 Seabrook, EYWTATCWIW, p. 25.
9 Seabrook, EYWTATCWIW, pp. 25-26.
10 Seabrook, EYWTATCWIW, pp. 26-28.
11 Seabrook, EYWTATCWIW, pp. 26-27.
12 Seabrook, EYWTATCWIW, pp. 26-27.
13 Seabrook, EYWTATCWIW, pp. 27-28.
14 Seabrook, EYWTATCWIW, p. 28.
15 Seabrook, EYWTATCWIW, pp. 25-29.
16 Seabrook, EYWTATCWIW, p. 29.
17 Seabrook, EYWTATCWIW, p. 29.
18 Seabrook, EYWTATCWIW, p. 30.
19 Seabrook, TAHSR, pp. 19-20, 84-86, 966-1001.
20 Seabrook, EYWTATCWIW, pp. 30-32.
21 Richardson, p. 430.
22 Seabrook, EYWTATCWIW, pp. 31-32.
23 Seabrook, EYWTATCWIW, p. 33.
24 Seabrook, EYWTATCWIW, p. 33.
25 Seabrook, EYWTATCWIW, p. 34.
26 Seabrook, EYWTATCWIW, p. 34.
27 Seabrook, EYWTATCWIW, p. 33.
28 Seabrook, EYWTATCWIW, p. 34.
29 Seabrook, EYWTATCWIW, p. 34.
30 Seabrook, EYWTATCWIW, p. 35.
31 Seabrook, EYWTATCWIW, p. 37.
32 See e.g., Seabrook, TAHSR, pp. 77-82, 213-217, 290, 322, passim.
33 Seabrook, EYWTATCWIW, pp. 47-51.
34 Seabrook, TAOCE, pp. 9-12.
35 Seabrook, TMOCP, pp. 237-238; Seabrook, AL, pp. 85, 91-95, 481.
36 Seabrook, EYWTATCWIW, p. 40.
37 Seabrook, L, pp. 215-246.
38 Seabrook, L, pp. 213, 225, 230, 243, 287.
39 Seabrook, TAHSR, pp. 323-324.
40 Seabrook, EYWTATCWIW, p. 46.
41 Seabrook, L, pp. 234, 905.
42 Seabrook, TAOCE, passim.
43 Seabrook, C101, pp. 39-40.
44 Seabrook, HJADA, pp. 82-92.
45 Seabrook, EYWTATCWIW, p. 47.
46 Seabrook, EYWTATCWIW, p. 47.
47 Seabrook, EYWTATCWIW, p. 48.
48 Seabrook, EYWTATCWIW, p. 48.
49 Seabrook, EYWTATCWIW, p. 48.
50 Seabrook, EYWTATCWIW, p. 48.
51 Seabrook, EYWTATCWIW, p. 49.
52 Seabrook, EYWTATCWIW, p. 49.
53 Seabrook, EYWTATCWIW, pp. 47-51.

54 Seabrook, AL, pp. 83-103.
55 Seabrook, EYWTATCWIW, pp. 52-53.
56 Seabrook, AL, p. 88.
57 Seabrook, C101, p. 61.
58 Seabrook, AL, pp. 91-92.
59 Seabrook, TAOCE, p. 17.
60 Seabrook, EYWTATCWIW, p. 53.
61 See Seabrook, AL, pp. 15-21.
62 Seabrook, EYWTATCWIW, p. 53.
63 Seabrook, L, p. 118.
64 Seabrook, L, pp. 120, 123, 124, 125, 129.
65 Seabrook, AL, pp. 47-50.
66 For more on this topic, see my book, *The Great Yankee Coverup*.
67 Seabrook, AL, pp. 293-318.
68 Seabrook, EYWTATCWIW, p. 54.
69 Seabrook, EYWTATCWIW, pp. 56-57.
70 Seabrook, EYWTATCWIW, pp. 55-56.
71 Seabrook, EYWTATCWIW, p. 57.
72 Seabrook, EYWTATCWIW, p. 57.
73 Seabrook, EYWTATCWIW, p. 57.
74 Seabrook, EYWTATCWIW, pp. 61-68.
75 Seabrook, EYWTATCWIW, pp. 61, 62.
76 Seabrook, EYWTATCWIW, p. 62.
77 Seabrook, EYWTATCWIW, pp. 62-63.
78 Seabrook, EYWTATCWIW, p. 63.
79 Seabrook, EYWTATCWIW, p. 63.
80 Seabrook, EYWTATCWIW, pp. 63-64.
81 Seabrook, EYWTATCWIW, p. 65.
82 Seabrook, EYWTATCWIW, p. 66.
83 Seabrook, EYWTATCWIW, p. 69.
84 Seabrook, EYWTATCWIW, p. 69.
85 Seabrook, EYWTATCWIW, pp. 69, 71, 72.
86 Seabrook, EYWTATCWIW, p. 69.
87 Seabrook, EYWTATCWIW, p. 69.
88 Seabrook, EYWTATCWIW, pp. 69-70.
89 Seabrook, AL, p. 385.
90 Seabrook, EYWTATCWIW, p. 70.
91 Seabrook, EYWTATCWIW, pp. 75, 78.
92 Seabrook, EYWTATCWIW, pp. 74-77.
93 Seabrook, EYWTATCWIW, p. 75.
94 Seabrook, EYWTATCWIW, pp. 76-77.
95 Seabrook, EYWTAASIW, p. 280.
96 Seabrook, EYWTATCWIW, p. 77.
97 Seabrook, EYWTATCWIW, p. 77.
98 Seabrook, EYWTATCWIW, p. 79.
99 Seabrook, EYWTATCWIW, p. 79.
100 Seabrook, EYWTAASIW, pp. 242-244.
101 Seabrook, EYWTATCWIW, p. 78.
102 Seabrook, EYWTATCWIW, pp. 78-79.
103 Seabrook, EYWTATCWIW, p. 79.
104 Seabrook, EYWTATCWIW, p. 80.
105 See Seabrook, EYWTAASIW, pp. 282-399.
106 Seabrook, AL, pp. 137-140.
107 Seabrook, EYWTATCWIW, pp. 81, 84-85, 86-87.
108 Seabrook, EYWTATCWIW, p. 85.
109 Seabrook, EYWTAASIW, pp. 425-426.
110 Seabrook, EYWTATCWIW, pp. 82-83.

111 Seabrook, EYWTATCWIW, p. 82.
112 Seabrook, EYWTATCWIW, pp. 90-91.
113 Seabrook, EYWTATCWIW, pp. 93-96.
114 Seabrook, EYWTATCWIW, p. 98.
115 Seabrook, EYWTATCWIW, p. 99.
116 Seabrook, EYWTATCWIW, pp. 99-101.
117 Seabrook, EYWTATCWIW, pp. 100-101.
118 Seabrook, EYWTATCWIW, pp. 109-115.
119 Seabrook, EYWTATCWIW, p. 109.
120 Seabrook, EYWTATCWIW, pp. 109-110.
121 Seabrook, EYWTATCWIW, p. 110.
122 Seabrook, EYWTATCWIW, p. 112.
123 Seabrook, EYWTATCWIW, pp. 112-113.
124 Seabrook, EYWTATCWIW, pp. 113-114.
125 See my book, *Honest Jeff and Dishonest Abe: A Southern Children's Guide to the Civil War*.
126 Seabrook, EYWTATCWIW, p. 116.
127 Seabrook, EYWTATCWIW, pp. 116-118.
128 Seabrook, EYWTATCWIW, p. 118. See also Seabrook, L, pp. 918-938.
129 Seabrook, EYWTATCWIW, p. 119.
130 Seabrook, EYWTATCWIW, pp. 116-132.
131 Seabrook, EYWTATCWIW, pp. 137-146.
132 Seabrook, EYWTATCWIW, pp. 129-130.
133 Seabrook, EYWTATCWIW, p. 147.
134 Seabrook, EYWTATCWIW, p. 133.
135 Seabrook, EYWTATCWIW, p. 133.
136 Seabrook, EYWTATCWIW, p. 133.
137 Seabrook, EYWTATCWIW, pp. 133-136.
138 Seabrook, EYWTATCWIW, p. 137.
139 Seabrook, EYWTATCWIW, p. 137.
140 Seabrook, EYWTATCWIW, p. 137.
141 Seabrook, EYWTATCWIW, pp. 137-138.
142 Seabrook, EYWTATCWIW, p. 138.
143 Seabrook, EYWTATCWIW, p. 138.
144 Seabrook, EYWTATCWIW, pp. 138-139.
145 Seabrook, EYWTATCWIW, p. 139.
146 Seabrook, EYWTATCWIW, p. 140.
147 Seabrook, EYWTATCWIW, pp. 140-141.
148 Seabrook, EYWTAASIW, pp. 690-691.
149 Seabrook, EYWTATCWIW, p. 141.
150 Seabrook, EYWTATCWIW, p. 141.
151 Seabrook, EYWTATCWIW, pp. 141-142.
152 Seabrook, EYWTATCWIW, p. 143.
153 Seabrook, EYWTATCWIW, pp. 143-144.
154 Seabrook, EYWTATCWIW, pp. 144-145.
155 Seabrook, EYWTATCWIW, p. 145.
156 Seabrook, EYWTATCWIW, p. 151.
157 Seabrook, EYWTATCWIW, p. 152.
158 Seabrook, EYWTATCWIW, pp. 67, 152, 174.
159 Seabrook, EYWTATCWIW, pp. 147-148.
160 Seabrook, EYWTATCWIW, p. 147.
161 Seabrook, EYWTATCWIW, pp. 147-148.
162 Seabrook, EYWTATCWIW, p. 151.
163 Seabrook, EYWTATCWIW, pp. 148-149.
164 Seabrook, EYWTATCWIW, p. 149.
165 Seabrook, EYWTATCWIW, p. 149.
166 Seabrook, EYWTATCWIW, pp. 154-155.
167 Seabrook, EYWTATCWIW, p. 155.

168 Seabrook, L, p. 94.
169 Seabrook, EYWTATCWIW, p. 158.
170 Seabrook, EYWTATCWIW, pp. 158-159.
171 Seabrook, EYWTAASIW, pp. 690-691.
172 Seabrook, EYWTATCWIW, p. 159.
173 Seabrook, EYWTATCWIW, p. 159.
174 Seabrook, EYWTATCWIW, pp. 159-160.
175 Seabrook, EYWTATCWIW, pp. 160-161.
176 Seabrook, EYWTATCWIW, p. 163.
177 Seabrook, EYWTATCWIW, p. 165.
178 Seabrook, EYWTATCWIW, p. 170.
179 Seabrook, EYWTATCWIW, p. 170.
180 Seabrook, EYWTATCWIW, pp. 170-171.
181 Seabrook, EYWTATCWIW, p. 171.
182 Seabrook, EYWTATCWIW, p. 171.
183 Seabrook, EYWTATCWIW, pp. 171-172.
184 Seabrook, EYWTATCWIW, p. 172.
185 Seabrook, EYWTATCWIW, p. 172.
186 Seabrook, EYWTATCWIW, p. 172.
187 Seabrook, EYWTATCWIW, p. 172.
188 Seabrook, EYWTATCWIW, p. 173.
189 Seabrook, EYWTATCWIW, p. 173.
190 Seabrook, EYWTATCWIW, p. 173.
191 Seabrook, EYWTATCWIW, p. 173.
192 Seabrook, EYWTATCWIW, p. 174.
193 Seabrook, EYWTATCWIW, p. 175.
194 Seabrook, EYWTATCWIW, p. 188.
195 Seabrook, EYWTATCWIW, p. 188.
196 Seabrook, EYWTATCWIW, p. 188.
197 Seabrook, EYWTATCWIW, p. 189.
198 Seabrook, EYWTATCWIW, p. 189.
199 Seabrook, EYWTATCWIW, pp. 189-190.
200 Seabrook, EYWTATCWIW, p. 152.
201 Seabrook, EYWTATCWIW, p. 196.
202 Seabrook, EYWTATCWIW, p. 196.
203 Seabrook, EYWTATCWIW, p. 197.
204 Seabrook, EYWTATCWIW, p. 197.
205 Seabrook, EYWTATCWIW, p. 198.
206 Seabrook, EYWTATCWIW, pp. 197-198.
207 Seabrook, EYWTATCWIW, p. 199.
208 Seabrook, EYWTATCWIW, p. 200.
209 Seabrook, EYWTATCWIW, p. 201.
210 Seabrook, EYWTATCWIW, p. 201.
211 Seabrook, JLOA, passim.
212 Seabrook, EYWTATCWIW, p. 201.
213 Seabrook, EYWTATCWIW, p. 202. For more on this topic, see my book, *Confederate Flag Facts*.
214 Seabrook, EYWTATCWIW, p. 203.
215 Seabrook, EYWTATCWIW, p. 203.
216 Seabrook, EYWTATCWIW, p. 203.
217 Seabrook, EYWTATCWIW, p. 204.
218 Seabrook, EYWTATCWIW, p. 204.
219 Seabrook, EYWTATCWIW, p. 205.

BIBLIOGRAPHY

Richardson, John Anderson. *Richardson's Defense of the South*. Atlanta, GA: A. B. Caldwell, 1914.

Seabrook, Lochlainn. *Carnton Plantation Ghost Stories: True Tales of the Unexplained From Tennessee's Most Haunted Civil War House!* 2005. Franklin, TN: Sea Raven Press, 2010 ed.

———. *Nathan Bedford Forrest: Southern Hero, American Patriot: Honoring a Confederate Hero and the Old South*. 2007. Franklin, TN: Sea Raven Press, 2010 ed.

———. *Abraham Lincoln: The Southern View*. 2007. Franklin, TN: Sea Raven Press, 2013 ed.

———. *The McGavocks of Carnton Plantation: A Southern History - Celebrating One of Dixie's Most Noble Confederate Families and Their Tennessee Home*. 2008. Franklin, TN: Sea Raven Press, 2011 ed.

———. *A Rebel Born: A Defense of Nathan Bedford Forrest*. 2010. Franklin, TN: Sea Raven Press, 2012 ed.

———. *Everything You Were Taught About the Civil War is Wrong, Ask a Southerner!* 2010. Franklin, TN: Sea Raven Press, revised 2012 ed.

———. *The Quotable Jefferson Davis: Selections From the Writings and Speeches of the Confederacy's First President*. Franklin, TN: Sea Raven Press, 2011.

———. *Lincolnology: The Real Abraham Lincoln Revealed In His Own Words*. Franklin, TN: Sea Raven Press, 2011.

———. *The Unquotable Abraham Lincoln: The President's Quotes They Don't Want You To Know!* Franklin, TN: Sea Raven Press, 2011.

———. *The Quotable Robert E. Lee: Selections From the Writings and Speeches of the South's Most Beloved Civil War General*. Franklin, TN: Sea Raven Press, 2011.

———. *The Constitution of the Confederate States of America Explained: A Clause-by-Clause Study of the South's Magna Carta*. Franklin, TN: Sea Raven Press, 2012.

———. *The Old Rebel: Robert E. Lee As He Was Seen By His Contemporaries*. 2012. Franklin, TN: Sea Raven Press, 2014 ed.

———. *The Quotable Stonewall Jackson: Selections From the Writings and Speeches of the South's Most Famous General*. Franklin, TN: Sea Raven Press, 2012.

———. *Honest Jeff and Dishonest Abe: A Southern Children's Guide to the Civil War*. Franklin, TN: Sea Raven Press, 2012.

———. *Give 'Em Hell Boys! The Complete Military Correspondence of Nathan Bedford Forrest*. Franklin, TN: Sea Raven Press, 2012 Sesquicentennial Civil War Edition.

———. *The Great Impersonator: 99 Reasons to Dislike Abraham Lincoln*. Franklin, TN: Sea Raven Press, 2012.

———. *Forrest! 99 Reasons to Love Nathan Bedford Forrest*. Franklin, TN: Sea Raven Press, 2012 Sesquicentennial Civil War Edition.

———. *The Quotable Nathan Bedford Forrest: Selections From the Writings and Speeches of the Confederacy's Most Brilliant Cavalryman*. Franklin, TN: Sea Raven Press, 2012 Sesquicentennial Civil War Edition.

———. *Encyclopedia of the Battle of Franklin: A Comprehensive Guide to the Conflict That Changed the Civil War*. Franklin, TN: Sea Raven Press, 2012 Sesquicentennial Civil War Edition.

———. *The Quotable Alexander H. Stephens: Selections From the Writings and Speeches of the Confederacy's First Vice President*. Franklin, TN: Sea Raven Press, 2013.

———. *The Alexander H. Stephens Reader: Excerpts From the Works of a Confederate Founding Father*. Franklin, TN: Sea Raven Press, 2013.

———. *Saddle, Sword, and Gun: A Biography of Nathan Bedford Forrest For Teens*. Franklin, TN: Sea Raven Press, 2013 Sesquicentennial Civil War Edition.

———. *Jesus and the Law of Attraction: The Bible-Based Guide to Creating Perfect Health, Wealth, and Happiness Following Christ's Simple Formula*. Franklin, TN: Sea Raven Press, 2013.

———. *The Articles of Confederation Explained: A Clause-by-Clause Study of America's First Constitution*. Franklin, TN: Sea Raven Press, 2014.

———. *Everything You Were Taught About American Slavery is Wrong, Ask a Southerner!* Franklin, TN: Sea Raven Press, 2014.

———. *Slavery 101: Amazing Facts You Never Knew About America's "Peculiar Institution."* Franklin, TN: Sea Raven Press, 2015.

———. *Confederacy 101: Amazing Facts You Never Knew About America's Oldest Political Tradition*. Franklin, TN: Sea Raven Press, 2015.

———. *The Great Yankee Coverup: What the North Doesn't Want You to Know About Lincoln's War*. Franklin, TN: Sea Raven Press, 2015.

———. *Confederate Flag Facts*. Franklin, TN: Sea Raven Press, 2015.

MEET THE AUTHOR

OCHLAINN SEABROOK, winner of the prestigious Jefferson Davis Historical Gold Medal for his "masterpiece," *A Rebel Born: A Defense of Nathan Bedford Forrest*, is an unreconstructed Southern historian, award-winning author, Civil War scholar, and traditional Southern Agrarian of Scottish, English, Irish, Dutch, German, and Italian extraction. An encyclopedist, lexicographer, musician, artist, graphic designer, genealogist, and photographer, as well as an award-winning poet, songwriter, and screenwriter, he has a 40 year background in historical nonfiction writing and is a member of the Sons of Confederate Veterans, the Civil War Trust, and the National Grange.

Due to similarities in their writing styles, ideas, and literary works, Seabrook is often referred to as the "new Shelby Foote," the "Southern Joseph Campbell," and the "American Robert Graves" (his English cousin).

The grandson of an Appalachian coal-mining family, Seabrook is a seventh-generation Kentuckian, co-chair of the Jent/Gent Family Committee (Kentucky), founder and director of the Blakeney Family Tree Project, and a board member of the Friends of Colonel Benjamin E. Caudill.

Seabrook's literary works have been endorsed by leading authorities, museum curators, award-winning historians, bestselling authors, celebrities, noted scientists, well respected educators, TV show hosts and producers, renowned military artists, esteemed Southern organizations, and distinguished academicians from around the world.

Seabrook has authored over 40 popular adult books on the American Civil War, American and international slavery, the U.S. Confederacy (1781), the Southern Confederacy (1861), religion, theology and thealogy, Jesus, the Bible, the Apocrypha, the Law of Attraction, alternative health, spirituality, ghost stories, the paranormal, ufology, social issues, and cross-cultural studies of the family and marriage. His Confederate biographies, pro-South studies, genealogical monographs, family histories, military encyclopedias, self-help guides, and etymological dictionaries have received wide acclaim.

Seabrook's eight children's books include a Southern guide to the Civil War, a biography of Nathan Bedford Forrest, a dictionary of religion and myth, a rewriting of the King Arthur legend (which reinstates the original pre-Christian motifs), two bedtime stories for preschoolers, a naturalist's guidebook to owls, a worldwide look at the family, and an examination of the Near-Death Experience.

Of blue-blooded Southern stock through his Kentucky, Tennessee, Virginia, West Virginia, and North Carolina ancestors, he is a direct descendant of European royalty via his 6th great-grandfather, the Earl of Oxford, after which London's famous Harley Street is named. Among his celebrated male Celtic ancestors is Robert the Bruce, King of Scotland, Seabrook's 22nd great-grandfather. The 21st great-grandson of Edward I "Longshanks" Plantagenet), King of England, Seabrook is a thirteenth-generation Southerner through his descent from the colonists of Jamestown, Virginia (1607).

The 2nd, 3rd, and 4th great-grandson of dozens of Confederate soldiers, one of his closest connections to the War for Southern Independence is through his 3rd great-grandfather, Elias Jent, Sr., who fought for the Confederacy in the Thirteenth Cavalry Kentucky under Seabrook's 2nd cousin, Colonel Benjamin E. Caudill. The Thirteenth, also known as "Caudill's Army," fought in numerous conflicts, including the Battles of Saltville, Gladsville, Mill Cliff, Poor Fork, Whitesburg, and Leatherwood.

Seabrook is a descendant of the families of Alexander H. Stephens, John Singleton Mosby, and Edmund Winchester Rucker, and is related to the following Confederates and other 19th-Century luminaries: Robert E. Lee, Stephen Dill Lee, Stonewall Jackson, Nathan Bedford Forrest, James Longstreet, John Hunt Morgan, Jeb Stuart, P. G. T. Beauregard, George W. Gordon, John Bell Hood, Alexander Peter Stewart, Arthur M. Manigault, Joseph Manigault, Charles Scott Venable, Thornton A. Washington, John A. Washington, Abraham Buford, Edmund W. Pettus, Theodrick "Tod" Carter, John B. Womack, John H. Winder, Gideon J. Pillow, States Rights Gist, Henry R. Jackson, John Lawton Seabrook, John C. Breckinridge, Leonidas Polk, Zachary Taylor, Sarah Knox Taylor (first wife of Jefferson Davis), Richard Taylor, Davy Crockett, Daniel Boone, Meriwether Lewis (of the Lewis and Clark Expedition) Andrew Jackson, James K. Polk, Abram Poindexter Maury (founder of Franklin, TN), William Giles Harding, Zebulon Vance, Thomas Jefferson, Edmund Jennings Randolph, George Wythe Randolph (grandson of Jefferson), Felix K. Zollicoffer, Fitzhugh Lee, Nathaniel F. Cheairs, Jesse James, Frank James, Robert Brank Vance, Charles Sidney Winder, John W. McGavock, Caroline E. (Winder) McGavock, David Harding McGavock, Lysander McGavock, James Randal McGavock, Randal William McGavock, Francis McGavock, Emily McGavock, William Henry F. Lee, Lucius E. Polk, Minor Meriwether (husband of noted pro-South author Elizabeth Avery Meriwether), Ellen Bourne Tynes (wife of Forrest's chief of artillery, Captain John W. Morton), South Carolina Senators Preston Smith Brooks and Andrew Pickens Butler, and famed South Carolina diarist Mary Chesnut.

(Photo © Lochlainn Seabrook)

Seabrook's modern day cousins include: Patrick J. Buchanan (conservative author), Cindy Crawford (model), Shelby Lee Adams (Letcher County, Kentucky, portrait photographer), Bertram Thomas Combs (Kentucky's fiftieth governor), Edith Bolling (wife of President Woodrow Wilson), and actors Robert Duvall, Reese Witherspoon, Lee Marvin, Rebecca Gayheart, Andy Griffith, and Tom Cruise.

Seabrook's screenplay, *A Rebel Born*, based on his book of the same name, has been signed with acclaimed filmmaker Christopher Forbes (of Forbes Film). It is now in pre-production, and is set for release in 2016 as a full-length feature film. This will be the first movie ever made of Nathan Bedford Forrest's life story, and as a historically accurate project written from the Southern perspective, is destined to be one of the most talked about Civil War films of all time.

Born with music in his blood, Seabrook is an award-winning, multi-genre, BMI-Nashville songwriter and lyricist who has composed some 3,000 songs (250 albums), and whose original music has been heard in film (*A Rebel Born, Union Bound, Cowgirls 'n Angels*) and on TV and radio worldwide. A musician, producer, multi-instrumentalist, and renown performer—whose keyboard work has been variously compared to pianists from Hargus Robbins and Vince Guaraldi to Elton John and Leonard Bernstein—Seabrook has opened for groups such as the Earl Scruggs Review, Ted Nugent, and Bob Seger, and has performed privately for such public figures as President Ronald Reagan, Burt Reynolds, Loni Anderson, and Senator Edward W. Brooke. Seabrook's cousins in the music business include: Johnny Cash, Elvis Presley, Billy Ray and Miley Cyrus, Patty Loveless, Tim McGraw, Lee Ann Womack, Dolly Parton, Pat Boone, Naomi, Wynonna, and Ashley Judd, Ricky Skaggs, the Sunshine Sisters, Martha Carson, and Chet Atkins.

Seabrook, a libertarian, lives with his wife and family in historic Middle Tennessee, the heart of Forrest country and the Confederacy, where his conservative Southern ancestors fought valiantly against Liberal Lincoln and the progressive North in defense of Jeffersonianism, constitutional government, and personal liberty.

If you enjoyed this book you will be interested in Mr. Seabrook's other popular Civil War related titles:

- EVERYTHING YOU WERE TAUGHT ABOUT THE CIVIL WAR IS WRONG, ASK A SOUTHERNER!
- EVERYTHING YOU WERE TAUGHT ABOUT AMERICAN SLAVERY IS WRONG, ASK A SOUTHERNER!
- THE GREAT YANKEE COVERUP: WHAT THE NORTH DOESN'T WANT YOU TO KNOW ABOUT LINCOLN'S WAR!
- CONFEDERACY 101: AMAZING FACTS YOU NEVER KNEW ABOUT AMERICA'S OLDEST POLITICAL TRADITION

Available from Sea Raven Press and wherever fine books are sold

ALL OF OUR BOOK COVERS ARE AVAILABLE AS 11" X 17" POSTERS, SUITABLE FOR FRAMING.

SeaRavenPress.com

www.ingramcontent.com/pod-product-compliance
Lightning Source LLC
Chambersburg PA
CBHW031609040426
42452CB00006B/452